BUSINESS
EXPLORER

THE BUSINESS EXPLORER

YOUR ROUTE TO SUCCESS

DAVE ROGERS

FOREWORD BY BRAD PARKES

THE BUSINESS EXPLORER
YOUR ROUTE TO SUCCESS
Copyright © 2024 by Dave Rogers

All rights reserved. No part of this publication may be reproduced, stored in a retrieval system, or transmitted, in any form or by any means, electronic, mechanical, photocopying, recording or otherwise, without the prior written permission of the author, except in the case of brief quotations embodied in critical reviews and specific other non-commercial uses permitted by copyright law.

Disclaimer: The information provided in this book is intended for general guidance and information purposes only. The views expressed are those of the author and should not be taken as professional advice. The author and publisher have endeavoured to ensure that the information provided herein is accurate and up to date; however, they cannot guarantee that no errors exist. The author and publisher shall not be liable for any loss, damage or expense arising from any access to or use of this book or any materials linked to it.

This book is sold subject to the condition that it shall not, by way of trade or otherwise, be lent, resold, hired out, or otherwise circulated without the author's prior consent in any form of binding or cover other than that in which it is published and without a similar condition including this condition being imposed on the subsequent purchaser.

A catalogue record for this book is available from the British Library:
  ISBN: [979-8-3232-8857-1]
  Subjects: [Business & Economics / Entrepreneurship]
  Classification: [658.4/21—dc23]
  First Edition 2024
  Independently Published via Kindle Direct Publishing

To my wife, Amanda, and our three loyal companions, Mollie, Charlie, and Winnie.

Thank you for the joy, love, and unwavering support.

This book would not have been possible without each of you.

In loving memory of Bertie,
Forever cherished, never forgotten.
I hope you are enjoying Rainbow Bridge.
July 2009 - April 2020

TABLE OF CONTENTS

Foreword 9
Introduction 13

SECTION ONE: THE GOLDEN COMPASS
1. The Happiness Equation 21
2. What's Your Why? 29
3. Blueprints for Success 37
4. Who Are You? 47
5. Navigating With Integrity 55
6. Developing Positivity 63
7. Finding Your Tribe 71
8. Sweat The Unsexy 81
9. Technology Talks 89

SECTION TWO: THE EXPLORER'S TOOLKIT
10. Embrace Your Imposter 103
11. Open Your Mind 113
12. Understand Your Impact 123
13. Better Working Together 133
14. Enduring The Storm 143
15. Mind Your Language 153
16. Your Competitive Edge 163
17. Navigating Daily Routines 173
18. Strength In Connections 183

SECTION THREE: BEYOND THE HORIZON

19. Your Future History 195
20. Scanning The Horizon 207
21. Worst Case Scenario 221
22. Disrupting The Calm 233
23. Mapping The Expedition 245
24. Building Your Crew 255
25. Streamlining The Journey 271
26. Charting Exceptional Experiences 283
27. Calibrating Your Compass 295

Afterword: Navigating Forward 307
Acknowledgements 311
About The Author 312

FOREWORD

"The danger of venturing into unchartered waters is not nearly as dangerous as staying on shore, waiting for your boat to come in." as quoted by Charles F. Glassman, is as pertinent today as it ever was.

If the pandemic taught us one thing during 2020 and beyond, it is that things are not as certain as we think they are, and there is often a need to navigate through waters previously unchartered or, indeed, waters that may be chartered but no longer accurate.

Businesses have always known the benefits of understanding the principles of change and the ability to adapt new ways of working, adopt new thoughts and principles, and seek to improve on previous ways of working. Tony Robbins says, *"If you always do what you've always done, you'll always get what you always got."* So, if you want to achieve different results, you need to do things differently; we must accept change to improve.

The journeys of famous explorers like Francis Drake, James Cook, and Ernest Shackleton and their peers, as well as more recent modern explorers like Leo Houlding, Joe Simpson, and Ranulph Fiennes, can teach us a lot about how we navigate the unexpected, adapt to changing conditions, and chart a route to success by being curious. Shackleton's experience is particularly interesting as he learned from Scott's endeavours, was curious about what worked and what did not, adopted some of Scott's ideas, and adapted some for the better, gaining improved outcomes.

So, how do we navigate our way through the unknown? How do we navigate better for improved outcomes through the known? How can we be more resilient in bouncing back from adversity and getting better outcomes?

Thankfully, Dave Rogers has the answers we need.

For years, Dave has been curious about what makes some organisations successful and why some organisations or projects fail. With his experience in various sectors and industries, he has a long-held desire to listen and learn, be open to change, and passionately help others do things better.

Dave desires to help businesses, organisations, and young people navigate their best course through his natural curiosity to map out routes to success from eliciting vision and revealing purpose to chart what success would look like. He is open to using all tools available, not being scared off, but embracing and adopting new ideas and different ways like the use of technology, Artificial Intelligence and the like, all to fulfil his desire to carve out success preparing for the known and expecting the unexpected and finding future-proofed solutions that can and will stand the test of time.

Whilst Dave has not circumnavigated the globe, led an expedition to the North or South Pole, or climbed a previously unclimbed face of a mountain, he is, however, a modern-day business explorer who learns from the past, considers the future, and delivers in these pages the benefit of his experience in his quest for everyone to achieve more.

I never cease to learn from Dave whenever we spend time in each other's company, and the same applies to this book, like his previous work. Dave has a knack for taking the complex and making it simple to understand and implement. I am confident you will learn much from these pages, as I have, that you can use to navigate your way through your challenges to achieve your vision and successful outcomes.

Enjoy your journey through this book and beyond.

Brad Parkes
Speaker, Business Consultant, and Author

INTRODUCTION

Have you ever wondered what drives human progress? What does it take to be a pioneer in your industry? What is the secret behind the success of thriving businesses? I believe the answer lies in exploration—the unrelenting curiosity to push boundaries and venture into the unknown. Whether it's Magellan crossing oceans or Neil Armstrong taking humanity's first step on the moon, explorers share a common thread: the courage to face uncertainty and the vision to see beyond the horizon. These same traits are essential in business.

As a business leader, you are an explorer, navigating uncharted waters in search of growth and innovation. Like the great explorers of history, your journey requires vision, resilience, and the ability to adapt. The business landscape is ever-changing, and the key to staying ahead is the willingness to embrace new ideas, test new strategies, and evolve with the times.

Over my 30 years as a business consultant, coach, and speaker, I've worked with leaders from all walks of life. I've seen the triumphs and the setbacks and witnessed what truly drives success. This book distils that experience into actionable insights, providing the tools to explore new possibilities, innovate relentlessly, and steer your business toward enduring success.

Let's embark on this journey together as a community of business leaders. We'll explore the principles of honest self-reflection, strategic thinking, and continuous improvement—all essential tools for any business explorer. These principles will help you align your goals, adapt to changing markets, and lead with confidence.

CALIBRATING YOUR COMPASS

The first step on any journey is knowing where you're heading. This means looking hard at your current strategies, operations, and objectives in business. Be honest with yourself—what's working and what isn't? Reflect on your reasons for change and consider the positive impact it could have on your business and beyond. Honesty and clarity about your intentions will be the foundation for the future.

EMBRACING NEW HORIZONS

Innovation is the fuel that drives exploration. To stay ahead, you must welcome new methods, ideas, and strategies with an open mind. This book offers a compass to help guide you, but it doesn't dictate your path. Evaluate what resonates with your goals, experiment with new approaches, and be willing to adapt. Your openness to new ideas will unlock profound business changes and excite you to embrace change and new possibilities, igniting a sense of adventure and optimism.

TURNING INSIGHT INTO IMPACT

It's not enough to gather insights—you must act on them. Understanding why specific strategies are crucial to your business success will motivate you to implement them. Successful businesses continuously assess and tweak their strategies, staying proactive rather than reactive. This process helps you spot trends, identify opportunities, and refine your approach, making you feel more in tune with your business and proactive in your decision-making, instilling a sense of control and empowerment.

The companies that thrive in today's competitive market aren't just the ones with the best ideas—they're the ones that act on those ideas. Look at Google, a company that turns its data-driven insights into constant innovation, or Tesco, which leverages customer data to enhance the shopping experience and drive operational efficiency. They don't just understand the market; they take decisive action based on that understanding.

LEADING THE WAY

Visionary leaders throughout history have demonstrated the power of exploration and action. One compelling example comes from Walt Disney, who revolutionised the entertainment industry by transforming imaginative ideas into real-world experiences. In his early career, Disney faced significant setbacks, including bankruptcy and losing creative rights to some of his earliest characters. Yet, instead of being deterred, he saw these obstacles as opportunities to innovate.

Disney's unrelenting drive led him to create iconic characters like *Mickey Mouse* and pioneer the first full-length animated film, *Snow White and the Seven Dwarfs*, which became a massive success against all odds. However, perhaps Disney's most significant leap came with his vision for *Disneyland*. At a time when the idea of an immersive theme park was unheard of, Disney dared to dream big. His passion for storytelling and his ability to anticipate the needs and desires of his audience enabled him to turn a seemingly impossible vision into a reality. *Disneyland's* opening in 1955 marked the birth of an entirely new concept—an entertainment experience that blended fantasy with real-life adventure.

Walt Disney's story exemplifies how visionary leaders navigate uncertainty and push boundaries. Disney redefined the entertainment industry by combining creativity, resilience, and a deep understanding of what drives human emotions and set a new standard for business innovation. His journey serves as a reminder that authentic leadership is not just about responding to challenges but about daring to imagine new possibilities and having the courage to bring them to life.

The experiences and lessons shared in this book aren't limited to traditional historical references; they remain highly relevant in today's business environment. Each chapter will delve into the stories of modern-day leaders who exemplify the principles we discuss, showing you how these timeless ideas continue to shape the success of businesses today. By examining the strategies and approaches of contemporary pioneers, you'll gain actionable insights that will help you apply these lessons to your journey.

NAVIGATING REFLECTIONS

As you journey through this book, take the time to reflect on your experiences. What strategies resonate with you? What actions will you take to implement these ideas? Keep notes in the margins and download the FREE workbook on my website to track your progress.

   https://shorturl.at/aBy6d

Embrace each chapter as an opportunity to explore new territories of knowledge and apply what you've learned. This book is your companion, helping you navigate the uncertainties of the business world with confidence and clarity.

YOUR ROUTE TO SUCCESS

Knowledge is just the beginning; success comes from applying that knowledge consistently and effectively. As you close this chapter, remember you are a passive reader and an active explorer. Your business journey is ongoing, and the direction you take from here will shape your company's future.

LET THE EXPLORATION BEGIN.

SECTION ONE

THE GOLDEN COMPASS

1. THE HAPPINESS EQUATION

Why do we chase success so relentlessly? Is it for wealth, recognition, or perhaps the promise of happiness? These questions often linger in the minds of many ambitious individuals. As you pursue your career and personal goals, you're frequently confronted with societal benchmarks that define success. But chasing these external goals can lead to a paradox: the more you achieve, the more elusive true satisfaction becomes. You might sacrifice your time and wellbeing in your relentless pursuit of success. Traditional markers of success—promotions, high salaries, and social status—are easy targets for validation but can obscure the deeper, more meaningful aspects of a fulfilled life.

The disconnect between societal definitions of success and individual fulfilment warrants deeper examination. Real success isn't about attaining what others deem necessary but discovering what genuinely brings you joy and contentment.

LEADING THE WAY

In navigating the complexity of success, it's inspiring to look at those who have walked the path before us, embracing a vision of success beyond the traditional. Whitney Wolfe Herd, the dynamic CEO and founder of Bumble is a shining example of how aligning your professional pursuits with your values can lead to a more fulfilling and impactful life.

Whitney Wolfe Herd: Building Success on Her Terms

Whitney Wolfe Herd's story is about resilience, courage, and a relentless commitment to her values. At the age of 35, Wolfe Herd has achieved what many might see as the pinnacle of business success: founding and leading a billion-dollar company that has revolutionised the world of online dating. But for Wolfe Herd, success has never been about just the numbers. It's about creating a positive impact and building a business that reflects her deepest values.

After co-founding Tinder, Wolfe Herd faced a challenging and painful departure, marked by personal disagreements and a high-profile lawsuit. It was a moment that could have defined her career in the most traditional sense: a successful young entrepreneur facing public scrutiny and adversity. But Wolfe Herd chose to redefine this moment, not as a setback but as an opportunity to build something new that aligned with her vision of a more inclusive, empowering world.

Redefining Success: Empowerment Over Profit

With the founding of Bumble, Wolfe Herd set out to do more than create another dating app. She wanted to build a platform that would empower women, flipping the script on the traditional dynamics of online dating. At Bumble, women make the first move, a simple yet revolutionary idea that challenges outdated gender norms and promotes relationship equality.

But her vision didn't stop there. Wolfe Herd expanded Bumble's mission to foster a culture of kindness, respect, and safety in dating, professional networking, and friendship. This broader focus led to *Bumble BFF* and *Bumble Bizz*, features that empower users to build meaningful connections in all areas of their lives.

Wolfe Herd's approach to business is a powerful reminder that success is not just about what you achieve but how you achieve it.

By prioritising empowerment, safety, and respect, she has built a brand that resonates deeply with millions of users worldwide. Her success story is more than just a booming business; it's about creating a platform that reflects her values and inspires others to do the same.

NAVIGATING THE WHY

Extensive scientific research supports the link between personal fulfilment and professional success. The well-known hedonic treadmill theory suggests that pursuits solely focused on wealth or status may offer temporary happiness but often lead to long-term dissatisfaction. This evidence-based understanding guides you toward a more fulfilling and successful career path.

Recent advancements in neuroscience have shown how personal fulfilment influences professional success. Engaging in work that resonates with your passions does more than make day-to-day tasks enjoyable—it activates your brain's reward pathways, similar to activities like eating your favourite foods or participating in a hobby. This activation releases neurotransmitters like dopamine and serotonin, which are associated with happiness and wellbeing, highlighting the intricate relationship between your passions and professional success.

These neurotransmitters elevate mood and enhance cognitive functions such as memory, attention, and creative problem-solving. Regular activation of these pathways reinforces the neural circuits associated with those tasks, making them more efficient and pleasurable over time. This creates a virtuous cycle where work becomes inherently rewarding, fostering a state of flow—a highly focused mental state conducive to productivity. Aligning work with personal passion can lead to sustained improvements in mental health and overall life satisfaction.

IT'S NOT ALL PLAIN SAILING

Embracing a new definition of success that prioritises personal happiness and fulfilment alongside traditional achievements poses significant challenges. These hurdles come from societal pressures and personal beliefs, influencing how you perceive and pursue success. Understanding these challenges is the first step towards overcoming them and redefining what success means in your life.

Cognitive Bias

While your brain is powerful, it's also susceptible to cognitive biases that skew your perceptions and decision-making processes. One such bias, confirmation bias, leads you to favour information that confirms preexisting beliefs or values. In the context of success, this can result in a narrow focus on traditional markers, such as high salaries and prestigious titles, often at the expense of what genuinely makes you happy. By recognising and actively countering these biases, you can broaden your definition of success to include factors contributing to personal fulfilment.

Understanding how cognitive biases affect decisions can empower you to make choices more aligned with your true desires and values rather than merely following societal expectations. Techniques such as mindful reflection, seeking diverse opinions, and considering long-term consequences can help mitigate the impact of these biases.

Societal Norms

It's a familiar story for many of us. Societal pressures often glorify a narrow view of success, emphasising wealth, power, and status as the ultimate goals. This conventional success narrative is perpetuated through media, cultural norms, and even the education system, creating a robust external environment that can make pursuing a less traditional path difficult.

The advent of social media has further intensified these societal pressures. By constantly showcasing the highlights of others' professional and personal lives, these platforms often lead you to compare your behind-the-scenes struggles with others' curated success stories. The result is unrealistic standards and unnecessary stress.

In addition, many cultures have deeply ingrained beliefs about what constitutes a successful life, such as high-paying jobs, prestigious titles, or visible signs of wealth. These societal expectations can overshadow personal satisfaction or creative achievements that might be more fulfilling, making it challenging to pursue a path that aligns with your passions and values.

Fear of Failure

Traditional paths offer a clear, socially validated roadmap, whereas pursuing personal fulfilment can seem uncertain and risky. Stepping out of your comfort zone to pursue what truly brings joy can be daunting. The lack of a clear path or roadmap for success when following your passions can lead to hesitation and self-doubt. Redefining success requires a fundamental shift in self-perception, which can be uncomfortable and challenging.

YOUR ROUTE TO SUCCESS

Crafting a fulfilling pathway to success requires a deliberate and thoughtful approach that moves beyond conventional goal setting and achievement frameworks. Here are some methods for integrating personal values and passions into your professional life.

Self-Discovery

Embarking on a journey of self-discovery is a crucial step in aligning your professional pursuits with your core values. This process involves uncovering your strengths, passions, and principles and discovering new aspects of yourself and your potential. Use guided introspections, personality assessments, and creative exercises to peel back the layers of societal expectations and reveal your true aspirations. This empowers you to redefine success on your terms, setting the foundation for a fulfilling career and shaping your success story.

Purpose-Driven Goals

Understanding your intrinsic motivations and setting goals that resonate with these insights is critical. Traditional goal setting often focuses solely on outcomes, such as achieving a particular position or income level. However, purpose-driven goal setting defines success through personal satisfaction, positive impact, and being present in the moment, which can lead to a more fulfilling professional life.

Daily Practices

Integrate happiness into your professional life through consistent daily practices. Make room each day for actions and decisions that align with your definition of success and happiness. Identify and incorporate activities that bring joy into your daily routine, such as starting your day with breathwork, walking to reconnect with nature, or dedicating time to read or engage in a creative hobby. These practices can enhance your wellbeing and foster a more fulfilling life experience.

Maintaining Direction

Maintaining a balanced approach to success, where happiness harmonises with achievements, requires ongoing effort and a commitment to personal growth. Sustaining your focus isn't just about persistence but creating a supportive ecosystem around your new goals. This will help you remain committed to your vision of success, ensuring that your daily actions reflect your deepest values and aspirations.

Continuous Learning

The journey toward a redefined sense of success is both enlightening and challenging. Continuous learning is essential to staying aligned with your new goals, helping you adapt to changes and overcome obstacles. Consider keeping a daily or weekly journal. This practice isn't just about recording events; it's about reflecting on your experiences, emotions, and lessons learned. Journaling can help you understand your progress, recognise patterns in your behaviour, and clarify your thoughts and feelings about your journey.

Alternatively, consider starting a blog to document your experiences. This public platform can be a personal reflective practice and a way to engage with others on similar paths. Sharing your progress isn't just about offering insights to others; it's about building a community of like-minded individuals who understand and support your growth. It's a way to show that you're not alone in this journey.

Regular Review

Implement a system of regular reviews and adjustments to stay flexible and responsive to new opportunities and challenges. Be prepared to adjust your practices based on your reviews. If specific approaches aren't yielding the expected fulfilment, explore new methods. This flexibility is critical to finding and sustaining success in a way that continuously resonates with your values and happiness.

INSIGHTS FROM MY JOURNEY

The 2020 pandemic was a pivotal moment in my life, forcing me to reassess what success truly meant to me. For years, I had chased the traditional markers—career progression, financial rewards, and corporate recognition. But as the world came to a standstill, so did I. With everything on pause, I had the space to reflect on what brought me real fulfilment.

I realised that my definition of success had been too narrow, focused more on external validation than personal joy and professional fulfilment. The crisis pushed me to reconsider my priorities. I asked myself, *"What do I truly want from my life and career?"* It became clear that the work I was doing, while rewarding in some ways, no longer aligned with my values or the lifestyle I aspired to.

That's when I made one of the most significant decisions of my life—to leave the security of my corporate career and start my own business. It wasn't an easy choice, but it was the right one as I found a new sense of purpose by redefining success to include personal happiness and aligning my work with my passions.

2. WHAT'S YOUR WHY?

Have you ever considered how powerful passion and purpose can shape your business? They can transform company cultures, influence big decisions, and redefine how you interact with your customers and the community, bringing a sense of empowerment and hope for a better future.

Passion in business isn't just about excitement. It's a deep, sustained drive that powers your company's mission. This energy inspires innovation and creates a vibrant, engaging workplace culture, often becoming the foundation upon which you build your unique identity and strategies.

On the other hand, Purpose is why your business exists—going beyond just making money. It answers the why behind your business, grounding every decision in something more meaningful than profit. It's about creating a legacy and positively impacting the world, giving everyone in your company a sense of responsibility and pride.

LEADING THE WAY

Few leaders have been as influential when building a purpose-driven business as Yvon Chouinard, the founder of Patagonia. From the very beginning, Chouinard set out to create a company that didn't just turn a profit but actively worked to protect the environment. His philosophy was simple: businesses can and should be a force for good.

Yvon Chouinard: A Pioneer of Purpose

Yvon Chouinard's vision for Patagonia was never about chasing growth for growth's sake. He built the company on the belief that success means more than just financial gain—it's about positively impacting the world. From Patagonia's earliest days, Chouinard prioritised environmental responsibility. Whether it was through using sustainable materials, implementing fair labour practices, or taking bold political stands, he redefined what it meant to be a responsible business.

Chouinard also believed in the power of activism. For him, Patagonia wasn't just a company; it was a platform to drive real change. Through initiatives like the *1% for the Planet* programme, which commits 1% of sales to environmental causes, and the company's outspoken support for grassroots movements, Patagonia, under Chouinard's leadership, became synonymous with purpose-driven business.

Ryan Gellert: Carrying the Torch

Under Gellert's leadership, Patagonia has doubled its commitment to the environment. He's continued the fight against climate change by pushing for systemic change, supporting grassroots efforts, and even filing lawsuits against government policies that harm the environment. Like Chouinard, Gellert sees Patagonia as a business force for positive global impact. He has ensured that the company's activism is woven into every aspect of its operations, from supply chains to corporate governance.

Purpose Over Profit: A Legacy Continued

At the core of both Chouinard's and Gellert's leadership is the belief that a business's success should be measured not just by its financial performance but by the good it does in the world. Patagonia's mission statement, *"We're in business to save our *home planet,"* continues to guide every company decision. This ethos of purpose over profit, introduced by Chouinard and championed by Gellert, remains central to Patagonia's identity.

Chouinard and Gellert offer a powerful reminder of the impact of purpose-driven businesses. Their journey challenges us to ask ourselves: *"What legacy do we want to leave behind?"*

NAVIGATING THE WHY

Did you know that companies driven by purpose often outperform their competitors in the long run? It's no coincidence. This success is fuelled by higher employee motivation, better customer satisfaction, and a more substantial brand reputation.

Customer Loyalty and Market Differentiation

In today's crowded market, purpose sets you apart. Take Innocent Drinks, for example. They've built a loyal customer base by aligning with environmental and social causes that matter to their audience. It's not just about selling drinks; it's about connecting with like-minded customers who share their values. This connection fosters loyalty, helping the company thrive even during tough economic times when customers become more selective about where they spend their money.

Employee Productivity and Innovation

When your team understands and believes in your business's purpose, something unique happens: their work feels more meaningful. When employees feel their efforts contribute to a more significant cause, productivity soars, and innovation flourishes. People are naturally more creative and driven when they know their work makes a difference.

Operational Efficiency

Purpose-driven companies often experience operational benefits that can't be ignored. With lower employee turnover and stronger brand loyalty, these businesses save on recruitment and training costs while maintaining a consistent and powerful message across all communications. Purpose creates cohesion, and clarity filters through every part of the business.

Workplace Morale and Employee Retention

When employees feel connected to a greater purpose, they're more engaged, happier, and likelier to stick around. A workplace with a strong sense of purpose becomes a magnet for talent, attracting people who want to make a difference. This leads to a dedicated team fully committed to achieving the company's goals.

Brand Identity and Public Perception

Customers care about more than just your products. They care about how you treat people, the environment, and your impact. Companies that stay true to their values gain trust and credibility, strengthening their brand identity. This reputation attracts loyal customers and draws in investors, partners, and new opportunities.

Leadership Influence and Industry Standing

Purpose-driven leaders aren't just seen as successful businesspeople; they're seen as visionaries. Aligning your business with broader social or environmental goals sets you apart as a trailblazer. You're not just keeping pace with the industry—you're helping to lead its transformation. That kind of leadership doesn't just elevate your company; it influences the entire sector.

IT'S NOT ALL PLAIN SAILING

Embracing a purpose-driven approach is incredibly rewarding, but it's challenging. Increased employee engagement and stronger customer loyalty are excellent outcomes, but you'll likely face hurdles along the way—both internally and externally.

Identifying and Understanding Resistance

Change isn't always welcomed with open arms. Often, resistance stems from a lack of understanding or fear of the unknown. The key is to identify those who might push back on your purpose-driven approach and address their concerns head-on. Open dialogue is crucial here. By listening to their worries—whether about profitability, process changes, or simply the unfamiliar—you can reassure your team that this shift is positive.

To tackle resistance, focus on continuous education and clear communication. Explain the long-term benefits of adopting a purpose-driven model and involve your stakeholders. When people feel included and informed, they're more likely to embrace the change. Case studies from similar organisations can help illustrate the benefits, making it easier to get everyone on board.

Changing Established Corporate Cultures

Changing a company's culture is no small feat, especially in established businesses. It takes time, patience, and a clear vision. Start with small, purpose-driven initiatives in areas that can quickly adapt and gradually work towards more significant changes. This phased approach allows your team to adjust comfortably rather than overwhelming them with a sudden cultural shift.

As a leader, you're at the heart of this transformation. It's up to you to embody the change you want to see. Actively participate in the new direction, align your actions with your company's values, and openly discuss how your decisions reflect its purpose. When your team sees you leading purposefully, they'll feel empowered to do the same.

It's not just about providing training; it's about engaging your employees in meaningful conversations. Ask them what passion and purpose mean to them and how they can bring that into their day-to-day work. When employees feel valued and see themselves as part of the bigger picture, they're more likely to embrace and drive the new culture forward.

YOUR ROUTE TO SUCCESS

Having strategic insight and operational expertise is only part of the equation. You should also build your business on a foundation of clear purpose and genuine passion. It's these elements that genuinely energise and drive success. But it doesn't happen by chance. It takes thoughtful planning, consistent action, and a firm commitment to your core values.

Articulating a Clear Purpose

First things first, get your key stakeholders together for open discussions and brainstorming. These sessions are crucial for shaping a purpose that resonates with the leadership and the wider team. This collaborative approach helps create a sense of unity, ensuring everyone is on the same page.

Once you've got a solid idea of your purpose, craft a short and powerful purpose statement. It should clearly express why your business exists beyond just making money. Think of it as the heart of your business – something that's inspiring, memorable, and highlights your positive impact on your customers and the community. Ensure this purpose is at the core of your communications, from marketing materials to team training sessions, so it becomes part of your company's DNA.

Developing a Passionate Culture

Your company's purpose should shine through in everything you do—especially in the way you lead. It's not just about words; it's about action. Leadership should embody the company's values every day, making decisions that align with your purpose. When leadership is passionate, it rubs off on the whole team. Show your enthusiasm for the company's goals, and watch how it inspires those around you.

It's also important to create ways for your employees to connect with the company's purpose on a personal level. Consider setting up innovation labs for passion projects or launching volunteer programs that support meaningful causes. These initiatives make your purpose more tangible and help employees feel more connected to the mission.

Remember to recognise those who go above and beyond in living the company's purpose. When you celebrate passionate contributions, you're not just motivating individuals—you're setting a clear example of what passion looks like in action.

Embedding Purpose and Passion

Purpose isn't a one-time thing. It should be woven into every strategic decision you make. Make sure your business goals align with your purpose, and when new opportunities arise, evaluate them based on how well they support or enhance that purpose.

Communication is critical here. Regularly share how your projects align with the company's mission, and make sure both your employees and your customers understand the impact your work is having. Share stories and case studies that highlight this impact internally and externally.

Finally, keep the lines of communication open. Gather feedback from your team, your customers, and other stakeholders regularly. This will help you stay on track and make necessary adjustments. Develop metrics to measure how well your purpose drives your business, and use these to fine-tune your strategy over time. This approach ensures that purpose and passion remain at the heart of your operations.

INSIGHTS FROM MY JOURNEY

Understanding my why has always been central to my professional life, but it wasn't until I fully aligned my purpose with my passion that everything fell into place. One of the ways I've embraced this alignment is through voluntary work. Supporting a mental health charity and helping young people with career education has given me a more profound sense of fulfilment than I ever imagined.

Working with the mental health charity has allowed me to contribute to something bigger than myself, helping others improve their wellbeing and giving back to the community. It's reinforced my belief that businesses are responsible for supporting causes that make a tangible difference in people's lives. Similarly, mentoring young people in their career paths has been rewarding to use my skills to guide the next generation, helping them unlock their potential and pursue their passions.

These voluntary roles have strengthened my sense of purpose and enriched my business approach. They've helped me stay grounded and reminded me why I do what I do—balancing financial success with making a positive impact.

3. BLUEPRINTS FOR SUCCESS

Starting and growing a successful business takes more than a great product or service. It requires a solid foundation that defines who you are, where you want to go and the principles that guide you. This foundation is built on your Vision, Mission, and Values—three key elements that form the strategic core of any company. They guide your decisions, shape your company culture, and help you plan strategically. While often mentioned together, it is crucial to understand that each has a unique role.

Vision

Your vision statement isn't just a look into the future; it's a practical tool that can guide your long-term planning and decision-making. It should be more than inspirational—it should be a beacon that helps you navigate the business landscape. A well-crafted vision statement is aspirational and motivational, pushing your business to strive for something beyond the immediate horizon.

Mission

While your vision looks to the future, your mission focuses on the present. It defines your current purpose, detailing what your business does, who it serves, and how it serves them. Your mission drives your daily operations and decisions, reflecting the immediate actions needed to achieve your vision. It answers fundamental questions about your business's existence and day-to-day activities.

Values

Values are more than principles and standards; they are the core of your company's culture and ethos. They foster a sense of belonging and shared purpose among your team when clearly defined. Values guide your company's behaviour and decision-making internally and in the broader community. They align with your ethical compass, influencing everything from internal interactions to business dealings. Well-defined values ensure consistency and integrity, promoting unity and cohesion in facing challenges and making decisions.

By clearly defining and articulating these three elements, you set a strategic direction and provide security and stability. This ensures that every team member understands their role in achieving the overarching goals, instilling a sense of reassurance and confidence. They provide a roadmap that aligns everyone's efforts, ensuring that every step taken reflects your company's core beliefs and long-term objectives.

LEADING THE WAY

Building a successful business isn't just about creating products or services—it's about having a clear direction and staying true to your vision, mission, and values. No one understands this better than Holly Tucker, the inspiring co-founder of Not On The High Street and Holly & Co. Her journey proves that success comes from a foundation built on passion, creativity, and a powerful sense of purpose.

Holly Tucker: Empowering Small Businesses

When Holly Tucker co-founded Not On The High Street, she wasn't just launching a marketplace but creating a movement. Her vision was simple but revolutionary: to give small businesses and creative entrepreneurs the platform they deserved. Tucker believed the unique, handmade, and personalised products crafted by independent creators could challenge big corporations' mass-produced, impersonal offerings. Her mission was clear: to empower small businesses to thrive in an environment where creativity and individuality could shine.

Vision, Mission, and Values Driving Success

What made Not On The High Street so successful? It wasn't just the beautifully curated products but Holly Tucker's unwavering commitment to her vision and mission. Her vision was about more than just business; it was about changing the world of retail by giving creative entrepreneurs a voice. She envisioned a future where small, independent makers could compete with the giants by offering something personal, meaningful, and authentic.

Her mission—to help small businesses turn their creative passions into thriving enterprises—was at the heart of everything she did. It wasn't just about providing a platform; it was about supporting these entrepreneurs and giving them the tools, mentorship, and visibility they needed to succeed. And it worked—Not On The High Street became a household name, connecting millions of customers with small businesses and giving hope to many aspiring entrepreneurs.

However, what truly set Holly apart were the values she instilled in every aspect of her work. Creativity, community, and empowerment were not just words for her but the cornerstones of her success. She believed in the power of collaboration, lifting others, and creating a community where everyone could flourish.

These values shaped the company culture, fostered strong customer loyalty, helped build a thriving business and made a real difference in people's lives.

Inspiring a New Generation of Entrepreneurs

After the success of Not On The High Street, Holly's passion for supporting small businesses didn't stop. With Holly & Co, she took her mission even further, dedicating herself to mentoring and inspiring the next generation of creative entrepreneurs. She's become a beacon of hope for those who dream of turning their passions into profitable businesses, offering advice, encouragement, and, most importantly, belief in the power of small businesses to change the world.

Holly Tucker's journey perfectly exemplifies how a clear vision, mission, and values can drive business success and create lasting impact. She shows us that when you build a business on passion, purpose, and principles, the results go far beyond profit—they inspire change, foster communities, and empower others to follow their dreams.

NAVIGATING THE WHY

Understanding the psychological impact of well-defined vision, mission, and values is crucial. Research shows that when these elements are clear and aligned with your actions, they significantly improve employee engagement, customer relationships, and overall business health, highlighting their importance and impact.

Clarity and Direction

A well-articulated vision and mission give your team a sense of direction and purpose. This clarity reduces uncertainties about where your business is heading and what it aims to achieve, allowing your employees to align their career goals with your company's objectives. This clear direction is a roadmap for all strategic planning and decision-making processes.

Cultural Cohesion

Consistent values act as the glue that holds your organisation together. Strong core principles can foster a cohesive culture that unites your team under a standard banner. This cultural strength becomes particularly important during stress or change, providing a stable foundation for interactions and decisions.

Purpose-Driven Work

When your team understands and connects with your company's vision and mission, their work gains more meaning. This is especially important for today's workforce, which often prioritises meaningful work over other job attributes. When employees feel their work contributes to a greater good, their engagement increases, enhancing productivity and job satisfaction.

Reduced Turnover

With increased motivation comes lower turnover. Employees are less likely to leave a workplace where they feel valued and see a clear connection between their efforts and the company's goals. This stability helps maintain knowledge and expertise within your business and reduces hiring and training costs.

Brand Integrity and Trust

Values aren't just words on a page; they are the foundation of your brand's integrity and trust. When your values are communicated and demonstrated through actions, they build a strong relationship with your customers. In today's market, where consumers are more informed and have more choices, businesses that align their values with their customers' values tend to be favoured.

Enhanced Customer Advocacy

Values also play a crucial role in enhancing customer advocacy. Customers who trust and feel loyal to your brand are more likely to recommend your business. This advocacy can lead to word-of-mouth recommendations, social media endorsements, and positive online reviews, which are invaluable for growth. Companies with solid and value-driven brands often enjoy a premium in their market, allowing them to charge more based on brand strength alone.

IT'S NOT ALL PLAIN SAILING

Crafting your company's vision, mission, and values is vital in defining who you are and where you're heading. These elements set the direction and shape the identity of your business. But bringing them to life in your company's everyday workings can be challenging. The actual test lies in blending the idealism of these guiding principles with the practical realities of running a business day in and day out.

Navigating Diverse Perspectives

One of the first hurdles you might encounter is aligning the varied perspectives of your stakeholders. Whether it's your leadership team, employees, investors, or even your customers, each group will have its own set of priorities and visions for the company's future. This diversity is both a strength and a challenge.

Fostering open dialogue and involving everyone in decision-making is invaluable. This might mean holding stakeholder meetings, conducting surveys, or setting up feedback sessions where all voices can be heard. The goal is to gather various viewpoints and work towards a shared vision that resonates with everyone involved.

Finding common ground might not be easy and may require compromise. But this process is essential. More than that, it's an opportunity for strategic thinking and creative solutions to shine, inspiring and motivating your team. These are your allies, helping you align different interests while keeping your business's core objectives intact and focused. Remember, the stronger the consensus, the more unified and committed your team will drive your company forward.

Adapting to Market Realities

Your vision and mission often reflect where you want your business to go—they embody your ideal future. But sometimes, these aspirations seem out of sync with your current market conditions or economic trends. This is where adaptability comes into play, but it doesn't diminish the importance of your vision, mission, and values. They remain the guiding stars in the storm of market realities.

To keep your vision and mission relevant, you need to be flexible. Be open to reassessing and tweaking these statements as the market evolves, consumer behaviours shift, or new insights emerge. Flexibility isn't about abandoning your ideals; it's about staying aligned with your goals and the realities of the marketplace.

While it's essential to aim high, it's equally crucial that your vision and mission are grounded in what's achievable. This means setting realistic goals, defining clear timelines, and establishing measurable objectives that connect your aspirations with practical steps. It's about turning your idealism into a roadmap that guides your business forward, ensuring that every step is purposeful and attainable, and keeping your team grounded and focused.

YOUR ROUTE TO SUCCESS

Your vision, mission, and values shouldn't just be words framed on the office wall—they're the living, breathing principles that influence every decision and interaction in your business. They are more than just inspirational; they must be practical, guiding you towards the future while helping you navigate the present. Building these elements thoughtfully is critical to creating a solid strategic foundation and a culture that aligns with your business goals.

Vision

Creating a compelling vision starts with the people who know your business best—your key stakeholders. Engage them in meaningful conversations to tap into their insights, aspirations, and expectations. These discussions are about capturing a shared vision for where you want to go, an ambitious and achievable future. A skilled facilitator can help guide these sessions, ensuring that all voices are heard and that the resulting vision reflects the collective ambition of your business. The goal? A vision that serves as a realistic beacon, lighting the way for all your business activities.

Mission

While your vision focuses on where you're headed, your mission is about what you're doing right now to get there. It defines your core purpose, your essential functions, and who you're serving. The mission statement should be clear and practical, showing how your business works today to achieve the future outlined in your vision. Keep it simple and relatable, something employees, customers, and stakeholders can understand and connect with. And most importantly, ensure it aligns with the bigger goals your vision sets out to achieve.

Values

Values are the heart of your company's culture—they shape how you do business and engage with everyone around you, from employees to customers. To define these values, bring your team together in workshops where you can identify the core principles that reflect what your business stands for. But don't stop at just creating a list of aspirational words; your values should be actionable, something your team can live by every day. Choose values your company can genuinely commit to and integrate into every part of your operations, making them a consistent guide for decision-making and behaviour.

Maintaining Relevance

As your business evolves, so should your vision, mission, and values. Keeping them relevant ensures they continue guiding your company in the right direction. The business world is constantly changing—whether it's shifts in the market, customer needs, or internal growth—so regular reviews are a must.

Create a structured evaluation process to assess whether your vision, mission, and values align with the current business environment. Involve a diverse group of stakeholders to capture different perspectives. This helps ensure your guiding principles remain meaningful and practical.

And don't forget—deeply embedding these elements into your company culture keeps them alive. Include them in your onboarding for new hires and offer regular training sessions to keep them in the minds of existing employees. When your vision, mission, and values are at the heart of everything you do, they will naturally shape your strategic direction and day-to-day operations, fostering a strong, cohesive, and adaptable business culture.

INSIGHTS FROM MY JOURNEY

Over the years, I've had the privilege of working with some genuinely exceptional businesses. One thing that consistently sets them apart is their commitment to revisiting their vision, mission, and values—not just when times are tough but also during periods of growth and success. It's easy to lose sight of these foundational elements when things are going well, but the most successful leaders know that reinforcing them becomes critical precisely in those moments.

These businesses don't just pay lip service to their vision, mission, and values. They communicate them clearly and, more importantly, embed them into their daily operations through specific behaviours and actions. I've seen first-hand how companies aligning their teams around these core principles can navigate challenges and opportunities with confidence and clarity. For instance, when a business is experiencing rapid growth or navigating an unexpected crisis, the leaders I admire return to their core principles. They ask themselves: *"Do our current strategies reflect our vision? Are we living our values in the way we're conducting business? Are the behaviours we're encouraging aligned with our mission?"* This constant recalibration ensures that everyone in the organisation works towards the same goals and upholds the company's integrity.

4. WHO ARE YOU?

Building a solid personal brand has become a must for today's leaders in a constantly evolving world. It's not just a career tool; it's an asset that influences your entire business. Your personal brand shapes your appearance by peers, competitors, employees, and potential clients. More importantly, it impacts company culture, moulds its identity, and reinforces its values, making you a key influencer in the direction and character of your business.

A well-defined personal brand does more than represent you as a leader; it acts as a lever for strategic influence and helps align your business with its vision, mission, and values. By aligning your personal brand with your business's core elements, you can drive your company toward success while fostering an environment that reflects your deepest values and aspirations.

LEADING THE WAY

Few leaders exemplify personal branding's power quite like Sebastian Siemiatkowski, the co-founder and CEO of Klarna. His journey from a small idea to revolutionising how people think about payments highlights how a personal brand built on innovation, boldness, and transparency can propel a business and an entire industry to new heights.

Sebastian Siemiatkowski: Financial Innovation

Sebastian Siemiatkowski isn't your typical financial services CEO. His personal brand is defined by daring to question the status quo by asking, *"Why can't payments be simpler, more transparent, and more customer-friendly?"* Klarna's buy now, pay later model has transformed how millions of people shop, but Siemiatkowski's personal brand has kept the company ahead of its competitors.

From the beginning, his vision was clear: disrupt the traditional financial services industry and make the world of payments more straightforward, flexible, and transparent for consumers. Siemiatkowski's willingness to take risks and challenge conventional thinking has become his hallmark. His personal brand speaks to innovation, determination, and customer empowerment. This bold approach has put Klarna on the map and turned it into a multi-billion-dollar company leading a global fintech revolution.

Redefining Leadership in the Fintech Space

Siemiatkowski's brand aligns seamlessly with Klarna's vision, mission, and values. His vision was to reshape financial services by creating a payment system that genuinely serves the modern consumer. Klarna's mission to simplify shopping and create more payment flexibility directly reflects Siemiatkowski's belief in making the consumer experience more intuitive and transparent.

But what truly sets Siemiatkowski apart is how he lives out Klarna's values. Transparency, customer-centricity, and innovation aren't just corporate buzzwords; they are at the core of every decision he makes. His leadership style encourages an open and forward-thinking culture where employees are empowered to think big and push boundaries. Siemiatkowski's commitment to transparency goes beyond his business practices—he has been open about his leadership challenges and growth, making him a relatable and authentic figure.

Siemiatkowski's leadership journey shows that a personal brand isn't just about what you achieve—it's about how you achieve it. His decision to build Klarna on the principles of simplicity and transparency in an industry often seen as complicated and opaque shows how powerful it can be to stick to your values.

NAVIGATING THE WHY

How you are perceived as a leader can significantly affect your ability to motivate and inspire your team. When your personal brand is authentic and authoritative, it enhances your influence, making it easier to mobilise resources, drive change, and achieve strategic goals. As a leader, your brand often embodies your business's values and ethos. A solid personal brand that aligns with these values can reinforce your business identity and promote a unified culture, boosting team cohesion and morale.

Your personal brand is also crucial for strategic decision-making. It ensures that your decisions reflect the business's long-term vision and mission, facilitating coherent and strategic execution across all levels. Understanding the impact of personal branding highlights its profound influence on leadership and company dynamics.

Psychological Impact

Research shows that leaders with clear and strong personal brands are perceived as more trustworthy and credible. Trust is not just a part of effective leadership but the cornerstone. Your ability to establish it is closely tied to the consistency and authenticity of your brand. When your personal brand is well-defined, it clarifies your communication, making your messages more predictable and understandable. This clarity enhances your ability to influence and guide your organisation because stakeholders are more likely to follow a leader whose motives and values they understand and trust. Leaders with engaging personal brands can create emotional connections with their employees and stakeholders, which are crucial for inspiring teams and driving them toward common goals, especially during times of change or adversity.

Sociological Influence

Personal branding also plays a significant role in sociological influence. How you are perceived affects your ability to build networks, influence others, and gain support for your initiatives. A consistent and authentic personal brand helps align your personal goals with your business objectives, facilitating negotiations and interactions. For instance, if you are known for your commitment to innovation and quality, you can garner support for new initiatives or improvements more swiftly. Leaders with strong personal brands are better positioned to leverage their networks effectively, which can be invaluable for achieving business goals and providing support, resources, and opportunities not available through formal channels.

IT'S NOT ALL PLAIN SAILING

Building your personal brand is not a straightforward journey. You'll need to navigate the complex dynamics of balancing public perception with personal authenticity and adapting to changes without compromising your core identity. It's essential to be prepared for these challenges and understand that they are part of the process.

Understanding Core Identity

One of the primary challenges in personal branding is maintaining authenticity while managing how others perceive you. You'll be scrutinised by various audiences—from employees and shareholders to the public—each with different expectations. In this context, a deep understanding of your core identity—what drives you and what you stand for—is crucial. This self-awareness serves as a compass, guiding you to adjust your approach while maintaining your brand's essence.

Expressing Your Values Authentically

You must find ways to express your values and beliefs authentically while meeting your audiences' expectations. This can involve making tough decisions that balance personal integrity with professional obligations. Ensuring consistency across various platforms and interactions is vital. Discrepancies between what you say and what you do can quickly undermine your credibility and brand authenticity.

Adapting Without Compromising Core Values

Adapting without compromising your core values is critical to staying relevant in changing business environments. You must adjust your strategies and approaches as business circumstances and market conditions evolve. However, adapting doesn't mean losing sight of your personal brand's core identity. Flexibility in your strategy and leadership styles is essential for responding to new challenges and opportunities. However, this flexibility should not come at the cost of your fundamental values and principles.

YOUR ROUTE TO SUCCESS

Cultivating a personal brand is essential for any leader aiming to positively impact and forge meaningful connections in their industry. We have seen that your personal brand reflects your values, beliefs, and priorities. It communicates to employees, partners, and the market what you stand for and how you approach your role. Developing a solid personal brand involves several strategic steps: identifying core values, effectively communicating these values, and maintaining consistency in all your actions and communications.

Identifying Core Values

Begin by identifying and clarifying your core values. These values form the foundation of your personal brand, guiding your decisions and behaviours. They should resonate deeply with your genuine beliefs and align with your business's culture and values to ensure coherence and integrity in your actions. Self-reflection or working with a coach can be invaluable in defining these values. Reflect on past instances where you felt most fulfilled or effective and analyse the underlying values driving those successes.

Communicating Your Brand

Once you've identified your core values, the next step is communicating them effectively. This communication extends beyond formal settings like speeches or presentations; it encompasses all interactions within and outside the business. Seize opportunities for public speaking, interviews, and media appearances to articulate your personal brand clearly and powerfully. These platforms offer a broad reach and can significantly shape public perception.

Maintaining an active and thoughtful presence on social media and professional networks is essential. Posts, blogs, and articles allow you to continuously express your values and insights, connecting with a broader audience. However, the most powerful communication of your brand comes from daily interactions. How you handle meetings, respond to emails, and engage with staff at all levels conveys your values and personal brand more effectively than any formal communication.

Consistency is Key

The strength of your personal brand depends mainly on consistency. Consistency in words and actions reassures others of your reliability and commitment to your values, fostering trust and loyalty. Strive to be consistent in your leadership style, ensuring that your decisions and behaviours reflect your stated values. This consistency builds a predictable pattern that employees and collaborators can rely on. Regular feedback from peers, mentors, and team members can help you assess the consistency of your brand. Self-assessment tools and periodic reviews of personal actions versus stated values are also beneficial for maintaining alignment.

INSIGHTS FROM MY JOURNEY

It has taken me many years to develop a personal brand that feels truly authentic to my values. Like many others, I struggled to define myself as a leader and what I wanted to represent early in my career. The journey of self-discovery wasn't always straightforward, but over time; I realised that my personal brand had to reflect my professional goals and the core values that drive me.

Aligning my personal brand with my values has opened countless doors. Opportunities I never expected began to materialise as I became more intentional about presenting myself in the broader business community. I've been fortunate enough to experience some truly unique moments along the way, and perhaps even more valuable has been the network of like-minded people I've connected with. These relationships have enriched my personal and professional life, providing me with collaboration, mentorship, and inspiration.

By staying true to myself and my values, I've built a personal brand that resonates with others and attracts new opportunities. This experience has taught me that authenticity is the key to creating lasting relationships and achieving meaningful and sustainable success.

5. NAVIGATING WITH INTEGRITY

Ethical leadership is more crucial than ever in a world of rapid globalisation and digital transparency. It's not just about hitting business targets but also considering the broader impact of your decisions on employees, shareholders, and communities. When you weave ethical considerations into your company culture, you set high standards that promote accountability and build trust. This trust boosts internal morale and loyalty and establishes a solid public image aligned with the values of transparency and social responsibility that today's consumers, regulators, and communities demand.

Drawing from earlier chapters, it's clear that ethical leadership isn't just a personal trait; it influences every aspect of your company. Ethical leaders embody their business's core values, turning personal integrity into strategy and operations. This alignment ensures that your business activities and goals are legally compliant and ethically sound, showing a deep commitment to doing what is right beyond what is profitable or convenient.

LEADING THE WAY

Jesper Brodin, the CEO of Ingka Group, the parent company of IKEA, exemplifies what it means to lead with integrity, purpose, and sustainability. Under his guidance, IKEA has evolved into a global force for environmental responsibility and social justice, proving that businesses can succeed while positively impacting the world. Brodin's leadership is a testament to the power of doing what's right for people and the planet while maintaining commercial success.

Jesper Brodin: Leading Ethically

Jesper Brodin has taken IKEA's commitment to sustainability and ethical leadership to new heights. Under his tenure, IKEA has become more than just a furniture giant; it's now a global leader in the fight for environmental sustainability and social responsibility. Brodin's leadership is built on transparency, fairness, and a profound responsibility towards his team and the environment. For him, business is not just about profit margins—it's about using the power of a global company to make a positive impact.

Brodin's vision for IKEA is bold: by 2030, he aims to use only renewable or recycled materials in all its products. His mission goes beyond environmental sustainability, creating a circular economy that reduces waste and maximises resource efficiency. His commitment to ethical leadership doesn't just stop at sustainability—it extends to fair treatment of workers, diversity and inclusion initiatives, and responsible sourcing practices.

Creating Lasting Change

What makes Jesper Brodin's leadership so inspiring is his unwavering belief that businesses must take the lead in creating a better future. His vision of a more sustainable world is not just an aspiration; it's a plan actively implemented across IKEA's global operations. Brodin has turned IKEA's values—sustainability, affordability, and inclusivity—into the driving force behind every company decision.

His leadership has transformed IKEA into a model for how large corporations can act ethically while remaining profitable. Brodin has shown that business and ethics are not mutually exclusive by pushing the boundaries of what's possible. His commitment to transparency—whether about the company's sustainability goals or its approach to labour practices—has earned IKEA widespread respect and customer loyalty.

NAVIGATING THE WHY

Ethical leadership isn't just a buzzword; it's backed by both psychological and organisational research, proving its importance for individual morale and the health of the entire business.

Boosting Employee Morale and Job Satisfaction

When leaders prioritise transparency, fairness, and respect, they create an environment where people feel valued. Research shows that when employees trust their leaders to act with integrity, they're more satisfied, engaged, and far less likely to jump ship—meaning lower turnover for your business.

Building Moral Congruence

When leaders and teams align on ethical values, it strengthens social bonds and fosters better collaboration. Ethical leaders act as role models, and this behaviour filters through the entire organisation, encouraging everyone to follow suit.

Fostering Trust and Safety

A safe and open work environment is one where people can speak up, share ideas, or disagree without fear. Ethical leadership creates this space, fostering innovation and agility because employees feel comfortable contributing and taking initiative.

Enhancing Customer Loyalty and Brand Reputation

Customers today care deeply about a company's ethics. Brands known for doing the right thing build trust and loyalty with their customers, and that loyalty is invaluable—especially in competitive markets, where customers tend to stick with companies that reflect their own values.

Ensuring Sustainability and Long-Term Profitability

Ethical companies often take a longer-term view, embracing environmentally friendly and socially responsible practices. This doesn't just help the planet—it can boost your bottom line. Avoiding shortcuts in product quality or labour practices builds trust with stakeholders, creating a foundation for lasting financial success.

Attracting Talent and Investment

Top talent and investors are drawn to companies with a robust ethical reputation. In a world where social issues matter more than ever, a business that leads with ethics can attract the best people and financial backing, especially those who want to support positive change.

IT'S NOT ALL PLAIN SAILING

As rewarding as ethical leadership can be, it comes with its fair share of challenges. These often arise from the complexity of modern business and the competing interests of various stakeholders.

Navigating Ethical Ambiguities

Ethical decisions aren't always straightforward. Sometimes, they involve balancing competing principles or making tough choices with no easy answers. This is where frameworks like utilitarian analysis (focused on the greater good), deontological ethics (based on duties and rights), or virtue ethics *("What would a good person do?")* come in handy.

Seeking Diverse Perspectives

Bringing diverse voices into the conversation can make all the difference when faced with tricky ethical dilemmas. Involving different perspectives—from an internal ethics committee, industry peers, or external advisors—can help you see angles you might have missed and lead to more informed decisions.

Overcoming Institutional and Cultural Barriers

Sometimes, ethical leadership clashes with an organisation's ingrained culture, particularly in industries where aggressive, results-first approaches are the norm. Promoting a shift towards ethical behaviour might meet resistance, but staying the course is essential.

Implementing Cultural Change

To truly embrace ethical leadership, you often need a cultural shift within the organisation. This takes time, consistency, and commitment. Start by modelling the ethical behaviour you want to see, reinforcing it through training and development programmes that embed these values at every level.

Aligning Ethics with Business Goals

Linking ethical behaviour to long-term business success is crucial for getting buy-in from stakeholders who focus on the bottom line. Use real-world examples of ethical companies achieving sustainable growth or reducing legal risks to show how integrity and profitability can go hand-in-hand.

Ensuring Transparent Accountability

Transparency is vital to maintaining trust. Set up transparent processes for addressing unethical behaviour and ensure everyone in the organisation knows how these systems work. Publicising these steps reinforces the message that ethical breaches won't be tolerated, helping maintain the integrity of your business.

YOUR ROUTE TO SUCCESS

Becoming an ethical leader is a journey that requires continuous learning and a strong commitment from you and your team. By making ethics the backbone of your leadership and business strategies, you can create an environment where doing the right thing is how things are done.

Cultivating Ethical Awareness

Like any other skill, ethical awareness can be developed and sharpened. Start by rolling out training programmes covering the legal and moral principles of business ethics. Interactive sessions, like role-playing or scenario-based exercises, can help you and your team practice handling complex ethical situations. Ethical leadership and corporate governance certifications are also great tools to keep you informed about the latest developments in business ethics and best practices. And don't forget to stay up-to-date on international ethical standards and compliance requirements, especially in today's global business environment.

Integrating Ethics into Business Strategy

Ethics should be woven into the very fabric of your business strategy. Use tools like decision-making frameworks, ethical decision trees, or stakeholder analysis to ensure your choices benefit your company and your employees, customers, and the wider community. Regularly reviewing stakeholder needs and concerns ensures that your business decisions are aligned with the greater good.

Promoting Transparency

Open communication is essential when it comes to maintaining trust with stakeholders. Be upfront about business operations, performance, and marketing efforts. Implement robust whistleblowing and ethical reporting mechanisms that protect anonymity and address concerns without retaliation. Creating an ethical culture isn't just about enforcing rules—it's about nurturing an environment where moral decisions are recognised and valued. When this kind of culture is built from the top down, it influences every part of the business, contributing to its long-term success, reputation, and resilience in the market.

INSIGHTS FROM MY JOURNEY

Throughout my career, the leaders who have had the most significant impact on my development have all shared one common trait: they led with integrity. Whether in their decisions or how they treated others, their commitment to doing what was right—even when it was difficult—left a lasting impression on me. These leaders taught me that integrity isn't just a nice-to-have quality; it's the foundation of authentic leadership and long-term success.

Reflecting on this more deeply while writing this book, I've realised something important: integrity attracts integrity. Over the years, I've noticed that you naturally attract like-minded individuals when you lead with authenticity and strong moral principles. The people who gravitate towards you, whether colleagues, clients, or business partners, share your values and commitment to doing things the right way.

This has been one of the most powerful lessons for me. Leading with integrity builds trust and respect and creates a network of individuals who inspire and support one another. This has been invaluable in my journey—not just for my personal growth but also for the success of the businesses I've been a part of. Integrity, I've learned, is the glue that holds everything together.

6. DEVELOPING POSITIVITY

Imagine a workplace where positivity isn't just about smiles and superficial happiness but a deeply ingrained culture that shapes every interaction. This kind of environment starts with genuine recognition and extends to supporting both personal and professional growth. Diversity and collaboration are celebrated, creating a sense of inclusivity where every voice is valued. This foundation of positivity boosts employee morale and productivity, propelling your organisation toward its goals with a motivated and committed workforce.

As a leader, it's crucial to be vigilant against negative influences that can undermine this healthy culture. Address bullying, gossip, and sabotage head-on, recognising how these behaviours can erode trust and cooperation. Navigating the complexities of organisational change is another essential aspect, as change often stirs anxiety and resistance among employees. By developing robust mechanisms to tackle these challenges, you can prevent negativity from taking root and spreading within your organisation. Influential leaders are the guardians of workplace culture in this environment. Your role involves fostering positivity and swiftly and effectively addressing negative behaviours that threaten organisational health. Through these efforts, you ensure that the culture remains vibrant and supportive, enabling every team member to thrive and contribute to your organisation's success.

LEADING THE WAY

When you think of developing positivity in leadership, Daniel Ek, the co-founder and CEO of Spotify, offers a powerful example of how a positive, innovative culture can transform a company and an entire industry. Ek has led Spotify from a disruptive start-up to a global leader in music streaming, and his focus on fostering a positive, growth-driven environment has played a vital role in this success.

Daniel Ek: Creating a Culture of Positivity

Daniel Ek's leadership at Spotify has always been about more than just music—it's about building a company where positivity, creativity, and collaboration are woven into the fabric of everyday life. Ek understands that to drive innovation, you need to create an environment where employees feel empowered to take risks, share ideas, and push boundaries. At Spotify, this culture of positivity has been crucial in enabling the company to stay ahead in a fiercely competitive industry.

Ek has built a workplace where everyone feels valued, and diversity is celebrated. He has fostered an inclusive culture by encouraging open communication and collaboration, where employees are motivated to contribute their best work. His leadership is rooted in the belief that a happy, inspired workforce is the key to creating a dynamic, innovative company. This focus on positivity has not only helped Spotify attract top talent but has also kept the company agile and forward-thinking.

Tackling Negativity and Building Resilience

Despite the fast-paced nature of the tech industry, Ek is determined to ensure that negativity doesn't undermine Spotify's culture. He recognises that issues like burnout, siloed thinking, and internal competition can derail progress if not addressed.

That's why he prioritises transparency, open feedback, and a continuous focus on personal and professional growth.

Ek's leadership style involves tackling challenges head-on while fostering resilience within the team. He has created an environment where employees feel safe speaking up about their concerns, asking for help, and learning from their mistakes. By encouraging this openness, Ek has built a culture that nurtures positivity and helps employees grow more robust in the face of challenges.

Leading Through Change with Positivity

Spotify's growth and evolution have required constant adaptation, and Daniel Ek has navigated these changes with a clear focus on maintaining a positive, supportive environment. Whether responding to industry shifts, managing internal expansion, or introducing new business models, Ek has consistently led with optimism and confidence, ensuring his team feels supported through every transition.

NAVIGATING THE WHY

Understanding the balance between positive and negative forces within a business is vital to solid leadership. These forces are always at play, influencing each other in ways that can either drive growth or hold the company back. By promoting positive behaviours, you can naturally push out negativity, while managing negative dynamics helps create space for positivity to thrive. Striking this balance is essential for creating a healthy, productive, and innovative work environment that can face challenges head-on.

The Science Behind Workplace Dynamics

Research shows that reducing negativity and encouraging positivity is crucial for optimising workplace dynamics. Negative behaviours like bullying, discrimination, and chronic complaining can drag down team morale and productivity, often leading to higher turnover. Conversely, positive practices such as recognising achievements, providing constructive feedback, and fostering supportive leadership boost engagement, creativity, and retention.

Optimising Workplace Energy

To keep negativity at bay, establish clear policies against harassment and discrimination, offer conflict resolution training, and encourage open communication where employees feel safe to speak up. On the positive side, celebrate team wins, give regular recognition, and build a culture where appreciation is part of the daily routine. These strategies improve morale and show employees their contributions are valued, aligning everyone with the company's goals.

The Psychological Impact of Negativity

A toxic work environment can affect an employee's mental health and job satisfaction. Continuous exposure to negativity often leads to burnout, anxiety, and low morale. Leaders can prevent this by promoting mental health awareness, offering wellness programs, and training managers to spot signs of stress or exhaustion in their teams.

The Benefits of Positivity

Positive psychology research highlights how a positive work environment makes daily tasks more enjoyable and helps employees tackle challenges with greater resilience. A positive culture expands employees' problem-solving abilities, leading to more creative solutions. It also fosters personal resources like optimism, confidence, and adaptability, which help employees manage stress, embrace change, and fully engage in their roles, creating a more dynamic and innovative organisation.

IT'S NOT ALL PLAIN SAILING

Changing a company's culture is no easy feat, especially if negativity has taken root. Some employees might resist, whether because they benefit from the current way of working or simply because they're sceptical of change. This resistance can take many forms, from passive non-compliance to open criticism.

Engagement and Inclusion

The key to overcoming resistance is involving everyone in the process. Ask for input from all levels and let people be part of the decision-making, giving them a sense of ownership in the new culture. Share success stories early to show the positive impact, and offer training and workshops to help employees understand and embrace the new values.

Overcoming Scepticism

Some employees may be cynical, especially if they've seen initiatives come and go without lasting impact. To counter this, be transparent and consistent in your communication. Clearly explain the reasons behind the changes and how they'll benefit the company and the employees. Keep everyone updated on progress and address concerns as they come up. Setting up a feedback loop where employees can voice their doubts and get responses can help turn scepticism into support.

Leadership Role Modelling

As a leader, your actions speak louder than words. By consistently modelling the positive behaviours you want to see, you set the tone for others to follow. When employees see leaders walking the talk, it helps build trust and reinforces the cultural shift.

Open Channels for Feedback

Create easy ways for employees to share their feedback and ensure they know their voices will be heard. Whether through one-on-one meetings, team discussions, or anonymous surveys, giving employees a safe space to express concerns and suggestions shows that feedback is valued and essential for improvement.

Actionable Follow-Up

Collecting feedback is not enough—what you do with it matters. When employees see that their feedback leads to real changes, it builds trust and shows that leadership is committed to creating a positive work environment. Keep the momentum by regularly sharing updates on actions taken in response to feedback.

YOUR ROUTE TO SUCCESS

Creating a positive, inclusive, resilient workplace culture takes intention and commitment. By implementing thoughtful strategies and continuous improvements, you can transform your organisation into a place where every employee feels valued and motivated.

Fostering a Valued and Inclusive Environment

Start by building an environment where everyone feels heard and appreciated. Encourage your team to share their ideas, concerns, and feedback through regular meetings, suggestion boxes, and open-door policies. Act on their feedback when appropriate, showing that their input truly matters.

Implementing Recognition Programs

Create recognition programs that reward employees for their hard work. This could be as simple as informal shout-outs during team meetings or as formal as an awards system. Recognition boosts morale and sets a tone of appreciation across the organisation.

Celebrating Achievements

Take the time to celebrate wins—whether completing a big project or hitting a key target. These moments of shared success strengthen team bonds and build a sense of collective achievement, boosting morale and motivation.

Providing Training and Development Opportunities

Invest in your employees' growth by offering training, workshops, and development programs. This will help them advance in their careers and enhance their contributions to the organisation, benefiting everyone.

Prioritising Employee Health and Wellbeing

Support your employees by offering flexible working arrangements, mental health days, and access to wellness programs. Initiatives like gym memberships or health workshops can promote overall wellbeing and keep employees happy and productive.

Offering Constructive Feedback

Encourage managers to provide constructive feedback regularly, highlighting areas for improvement while recognising strengths.

Move away from annual reviews and introduce more frequent performance discussions to give timely feedback and keep employees on track with company goals, fostering continuous development and growth.

INSIGHTS FROM MY JOURNEY

I've always been naturally optimistic, and this mindset has shaped not only how I approach challenges but also how I now run my business. When faced with a problem or a setback, I tend to focus on solutions rather than dwell on the negativity surrounding the situation. By staying optimistic and forward-looking, I've found that I can move through challenges with greater clarity and resilience.

This approach has helped me personally and had a noticeable impact on those around me. Over the years, colleagues and clients have remarked on how my positive outlook inspires them to adopt a similar mindset. It's not about ignoring the reality of a situation but about reframing challenges as opportunities for growth. Focusing on what can be done rather than what has gone wrong has fostered an environment where people feel empowered to act and find solutions.

I believe that positivity is contagious. When leaders show optimism, it creates a ripple effect, lifting the mood and motivation of the entire team. In my experience, this has been a powerful way to build stronger relationships, drive productivity, and create a workplace where people thrive.

7. FINDING YOUR TRIBE

Success thrives within a supportive community—this is your tribe. This group comprises customers, employees, and connections who resonate deeply with your brand's ethos and values. These individuals aren't just transactional; they believe in what you stand for and are emotionally invested in your success. For customers, this means connecting with those who need your product or service and feel a personal alignment with your brand's mission. For employees, it involves building a team passionately committed to the company's collective goals. Connections mean purposefully networking and seeking relationships to amplify your brand's reach and impact.

Cultivating this tribe requires ongoing effort and genuine engagement. It's about consistently delivering value, staying true to your brand's mission, and building trust through transparency and authenticity. This community of advocates becomes your brand's voice, amplifying your message and helping you navigate challenges. By fostering these relationships, you create a network of support that enhances your brand's resilience, drives growth, and ensures long-term success. A unified tribe propels your business forward through collective support and shared passion, making your brand more resilient and respected.

LEADING THE WAY

When building a thriving, loyal community around your brand, few have done it as effectively as Ben Francis, the founder and CEO of

Gymshark. What started as a small operation in his garage has grown into a global fitness phenomenon, thanks to Francis' ability to cultivate a tribe of fitness enthusiasts who love the brand's products and feel a deep connection to its ethos.

Ben Francis: Building a Fitness Community

Ben Francis understood from the start that building a brand wasn't just about selling products; it was about creating a community of people who believed in the same mission. His vision for Gymshark wasn't just to provide high-quality fitness apparel and connect and inspire fitness enthusiasts worldwide. This community-driven approach transformed Gymshark from a niche start-up to one of the fastest-growing fitness brands globally.

At the heart of Gymshark's success is a shared passion for fitness, innovation, and personal growth. Francis didn't just create products for athletes—he created an entire ecosystem where fitness lovers could feel like they belong. By aligning his brand with the values of dedication, perseverance, and continuous improvement, he cultivated a tribe that sees Gymshark as more than just a fitness brand; it's a lifestyle.

Leveraging Social Media and Influencers

Francis' strategy for building Gymshark's tribe was rooted in authenticity and connection. He understood early on that modern consumers, particularly those in the fitness community, wanted more than just products—they wanted to feel part of something bigger. Francis and his team engaged directly with their audience through savvy social media to sell and foster relationships.

He also built partnerships with fitness influencers who genuinely embodied the Gymshark lifestyle. These influencers, already admired by their followers, helped amplify the Gymshark message, creating a powerful sense of community among their fans. Francis didn't just use influencers for promotion—he made them part of the Gymshark family, aligning their brands with his company's values. This authenticity resonated with their followers, turning customers into passionate brand advocates.

Nurturing the Tribe

Francis' commitment to building a supportive and inclusive community extended beyond marketing. Gymshark's mission is to provide innovative, practical performance wear and inspire people to pursue their fitness journeys confidently. Gymshark's events, such as pop-up shops and fitness expos, allow the brand's community to connect in person, reinforcing that sense of belonging.

Internally, Francis has built a team that shares his vision and passion for the fitness community. Gymshark's company culture is rooted in collaboration, innovation, and positivity—values that mirror the brand's external message. By fostering an internal culture that aligns with the brand's mission, Francis has ensured that Gymshark's tribe—both inside and out—remains united, loyal, and dedicated to the brand's continued success.

NAVIGATING THE WHY

Your business's success depends on both your market presence and internal harmony. The goal is to create a seamless value chain where inspired employees create outstanding products or services, leading to delighted customers eager to engage with your brand. This alignment is crucial in forging a robust, resilient identity that can withstand market shifts and competitive pressures. Identifying and engaging with your tribe requires a thoughtful blend of analytics, intuition, and strategy. Understanding the intricacies of human behaviour and group dynamics offers invaluable insights into how businesses can effectively assemble and nurture their tribes.

Psychological and Sociological Insights

Group dynamics and organisational behaviour principles are at the heart of team management. Research in these areas examines how individuals function within a group and how these interactions affect performance and satisfaction. For example, studies have shown that teams with a clear sense of shared goals and mutual support exhibit higher productivity and better problem-solving capabilities. Understanding consumer psychology is crucial for developing effective customer engagement strategies. This includes exploring how customers make purchasing decisions and what emotional and cognitive processes influence these decisions. Insights into perception, attitudes, and motivation can guide the development of marketing strategies that resonate more deeply with target audiences.

Evidence-Based Strategies

Scientific studies consistently highlight the positive impact of team cohesion on organisational productivity. Cohesive teams are more resilient in the face of challenges and can navigate workplace stress more effectively. Incorporating findings from behavioural economics can provide a deeper understanding of customer engagement strategies. For instance, the concept of nudges—subtle changes in how choices are presented—can significantly influence customer behaviour in ways beneficial to both the customer and the business.

Application of Theories in Practical Settings

Maslow's *Hierarchy of Needs* can be applied to team management and customer engagement by understanding and addressing the various levels of needs. For employees, creating an environment that addresses basic safety and security while fostering esteem and self-actualisation can lead to greater job satisfaction and loyalty. For customers, marketing strategies can be designed to resonate with different levels of needs, from the functional (safety, utility) to the emotional (belonging, esteem). In employee engagement, Herzberg's *Two-Factor theory* distinguishes between hygiene factors (salary, work conditions) and motivators (recognition, challenging work). Ensuring hygiene factors are adequately met prevents dissatisfaction while maximising motivators enhances job satisfaction and productivity.

Exploring Branding and Customer Loyalty

Branding is more than just a marketing tool; it establishes and deepens emotional connections with customers. Research into brand psychology suggests that solid brands can evoke trust and security. Understanding how brands can become part of a customer's self-identity or lifestyle can help businesses cultivate loyalty and encourage long-term engagement.

IT'S NOT ALL PLAIN SAILING

As you assemble your tribe and cultivate robust internal and external relationships, you will inevitably encounter various hurdles. Effectively addressing these challenges is crucial for maintaining the integrity and growth of the company.

Recruitment Challenges

Attracting top talent can be challenging in highly competitive industries. Enhance your employer brand to make your company more attractive to potential employees. Showcase your culture, employee benefits, and career development opportunities through various channels such as social media, company websites, and job fairs to boost your talent acquisition efforts. Establish connections with universities, colleges, and vocational schools to tap into emerging talent. Internship programs and collaborative projects can serve as a pipeline for recruiting young, skilled individuals familiar with your company's operations and values. Consider non-traditional sources of talent, such as career changers or individuals returning to the workforce, who often bring diverse experiences and perspectives that can enrich your team.

Customer Engagement Difficulties

In saturated markets, customers have numerous options, making it difficult for your company to stand out. Focus on what makes your brand unique, such as an innovative product feature, exceptional service, or a solid sustainability commitment, and communicate these differentiators in all marketing materials. Target specific market segments with specialised needs that your competitors may need to address. Tailoring your products or services to meet these needs can help you attract a loyal customer base. Conduct regular market research to stay ahead of trends and understand changing customer preferences. This research should inform product development, marketing strategies, and customer service enhancements.

Flexibility and Adaptability

Cultivate a flexible approach to product development that allows quick response to new customer needs and market opportunities. This might involve modular product designs or easily adapted service offerings. By understanding your business's specific hurdles and implementing tailored strategies to overcome them, you can ensure your company survives and thrives in competitive and rapidly changing environments.

YOUR ROUTE TO SUCCESS

To drive meaningful engagement and growth, it's essential to understand your key customers and bring your teams along on the journey. This means deep diving into customer data and behaviour while fostering a culture that aligns your people with your mission.

Understanding and Engaging Your Customers

Start by getting a clear picture of who your customers are. Use quantitative research to gather basic demographic details—age, gender, income, location—alongside valuable insights from surveys, market reports, and analytics platforms. This will help you track purchasing patterns, preferences, and behaviour, allowing you to identify key trends and customer needs. But don't stop there. Dive deeper with qualitative research to understand the motivations, attitudes, and emotions driving their decisions. Blending both data types gives you a full 360-degree view of your customers.

Customer Segmentation

Go beyond the surface-level demographics and explore how people behave—look at their purchasing habits, brand loyalty, and how they use your products or services. This approach allows you to target specific groups more effectively, ensuring your marketing hits the right notes. Consider what each segment needs most, whether solving a particular problem or fulfilling a specific desire and tailor your messaging to address those concerns directly.

Personalised Marketing

This could be as simple as using their name in emails or as sophisticated as recommending products based on past purchases or browsing behaviour. Tailor your content to each group's interests, whether creating video tutorials for tech enthusiasts or detailed guides for those needing more information. Reward loyalty with special offers, discounts, or exclusive previews, and consider hosting events—whether online webinars or local meetups—to show appreciation and build a community around your brand. Keep the conversation going through newsletters, social media, and personalised emails to nurture long-term relationships.

Assembling a Supportive Team

Your team is the backbone of your company's success. Start by clearly communicating your organisation's core values and culture to attract employees who resonate with them. Incorporate these values into job descriptions and recruitment materials so potential candidates know what your business stands for and can decide if it fits.

Recruitment Strategies

When interviewing, focus on cultural fit as much as skills. Ask candidates to share examples of how they've handled ethical dilemmas or teamwork challenges to see how their values align with your company's ethos. Include a diverse group of current employees in the recruitment process to get different perspectives on cultural fit and help new hires feel welcomed and supported by the team.

Nurturing Team Dynamics

Once your team is in place, nurturing their growth is essential. Create personalised development plans that focus on their strengths and career aspirations—whether that's through external courses, industry conferences, or in-house training. Pair less experienced employees with seasoned mentors to help them grow professionally while reinforcing your company's culture and values.

Team Building

Organise activities that reflect your company's values to keep your team connected and engaged. These could range from community service projects that build cooperation and give back to creative problem-solving workshops that inspire innovation. Encourage open feedback through regular one-on-one meetings, anonymous surveys, or team forums so employees feel heard and valued. This transparency is key to maintaining a positive workplace and driving continuous improvement.

Cultivating Company Culture

Your company's values shouldn't just be talked about—they should be lived inside and outside the business. Suppose sustainability is one of your core values, for example. In that case, it should show up in everything from how you run internal operations (like recycling) to how you market and package your products. You build trust and strengthen your brand's reputation by ensuring consistency between your internal culture and external actions.

INSIGHTS FROM MY JOURNEY

Early in my career, I had the opportunity to work on launching a new hospitality brand, which has since grown to become one of the most successful in the UK. It was an exciting time, and as part of the development process, our team was encouraged to read *Raving Fans* by Ken Blanchard and Sheldon Bowles. At the time, the focus seemed to be on the customer—creating loyal, repeat customers who would become advocates for the brand. But as I reflect on it now, I realise *Raving Fans* applies just as much to the internal team as it does to customers.

Building a tribe isn't just about external relationships; it's about creating a robust and cohesive team that believes in your vision and values. The team's energy and passion directly influence the customer experience, and when your internal tribe is engaged, motivated, and aligned, that enthusiasm naturally extends to your customers.

This experience taught me that finding your tribe isn't limited to those who buy your products or services—it's also about building a community within your organisation. When you have a team that feels valued and shares your goals, it creates a powerful synergy that drives business success and fosters long-term loyalty from your customers.

8. SWEAT THE UNSEXY

It's easy to get caught up in the excitement of new ideas and rapid growth, often overlooking the importance of structured planning and solid processes. These tasks might seem tedious or restrictive. They are the unsexy side of business. However, not paying attention to them can lead to chaos, inefficiency, and failure. Imagine setting off on a journey without a map or adequate supplies. The risks and uncertainties would be overwhelming. Similarly, in business, planning and preparation equip you with the tools to anticipate and navigate challenges successfully. Effective processes ensure that your team operates efficiently, reducing wasted time and resources. By laying a solid groundwork through meticulous planning, thorough preparation, and efficient processes, you create a stable platform where creativity and innovation can flourish.

LEADING THE WAY

The story of Toys 'R' Us is a powerful reminder of how neglecting the unsexy side of business—planning, preparation, and robust processes—can lead to the downfall of even the most beloved brands. For many, Toys 'R' Us was a staple of British childhoods, a magical place where kids could explore aisles filled with toys, games, and possibilities. However, despite its iconic status, the company's inability to adapt to changing market dynamics led to its eventual collapse.

Toys 'R' Us: Failing to Adapt in the Digital Age

At its peak, Toys 'R' Us was the leading toy destination in the UK and worldwide. However, as the retail landscape shifted in the early 2000s, with the rise of e-commerce and changing consumer behaviour, the company failed to evolve with the times. Rather than investing in its e-commerce platform and building a digital presence, Toys 'R' Us partnered with Amazon, effectively outsourcing its online sales. While this seemed like a convenient solution at the time, it ultimately cost Toys 'R' Us valuable opportunities to innovate and maintain direct control over their customer relationships.

As online shopping became the norm and competitors like Amazon and Walmart ramped up their e-commerce strategies, Toys 'R' Us remained primarily focused on its brick-and-mortar stores. The company's failure to prioritise the development of its online platform meant it missed out on the digital revolution, leaving it vulnerable to more agile and tech-savvy competitors.

Lack of Strategic Planning and Process

The downfall of Toys 'R' Us wasn't just about the rise of e-commerce—it was about a lack of foresight, strategic planning, and processes that could have prepared the company for changing consumer habits. Instead of proactively responding to the digital age, they clung to a business model that was losing relevance. It was too late when they realised the importance of developing their e-commerce platform.

The company's failure to anticipate shifts in consumer behaviour, invest in robust digital processes, and reimagine its business for the future left it unable to compete in a fast-changing market. This lack of long-term planning and preparation ultimately led to the company filing for bankruptcy in 2017, potentially closing a chapter on a brand synonymous with childhood joy for generations.

The story of Toys 'R' Us serves as a stark reminder of the potential consequences of neglecting the less glamorous aspects of business—like planning, preparation, and processes. It's a powerful example of how even a beloved and successful brand can face failure. The lesson is clear: even businesses that seem untouchable must stay ahead by sweating the details, embracing change, and making intelligent, strategic decisions that ensure long-term sustainability.

NAVIGATING THE WHY

Planning, preparation, and structured processes are the backbone of high-performing, resilient businesses. These principles improve decision-making and lay the foundation for long-term success. By integrating these strategies into your operations, you create a business that's adaptable, efficient, and ready to thrive.

The Psychological and Organisational Impact

Structured planning takes the guesswork out of decision-making, reducing stress while boosting productivity and engagement. Research from the *Journal of Applied Psychology* shows that clear goal-setting and processes enhance performance and increase job satisfaction. When teams have a clear path, they focus better, feel more accomplished, and perform at their peak.

Psychologically, planning activates the brain's prefrontal cortex, which handles complex thinking, decision-making, and social behaviour. This helps you foresee outcomes, develop strategies, and feel more in control. By reducing uncertainty, structured planning frees up mental space, allowing for more creativity and innovation—two key ingredients in a dynamic and productive workplace.

The Power of Structured Processes

The Project Management Institute reports that businesses with solid processes are far more successful. High-performing companies achieve their goals 90% of the time, compared to just 36% for those with less-defined processes. Transparent, structured processes don't just make tasks more efficient—they empower employees, reduce mistakes, and build confidence across the organisation.

Processes also foster continuous improvement. When workflows are standardised, it's easier to spot inefficiencies and adjust. This helps businesses adapt to changing conditions while keeping a competitive edge. A clear framework also promotes accountability, ensuring everyone understands their role and how it fits into the bigger picture.

The Role of Preparation

Preparation is all about anticipating challenges and developing strategies to handle them. It's proactive, not reactive. With contingency plans in place, your business can tackle unexpected disruptions head-on, whether they're market shifts, economic downturns, or internal challenges. Training and development also play a significant role here, ensuring your team has the skills and knowledge to adapt to new demands.

Investing in preparation leads to resilience. Businesses prioritising preparation are better equipped to weather tough times, whether navigating competitive pressures or internal disruptions. Plus, this readiness strengthens customer trust and loyalty, as clients can rely on your business to consistently meet their needs.

IT'S NOT ALL PLAIN SAILING

Even with the best-laid plans, the journey to business success is rarely smooth sailing. Challenges arise—some expected, others completely unforeseen—that test your ability to adapt, innovate, and stay on course. During these moments, the strength of your planning, preparation, and processes is revealed.

Overcoming Cultural Resistance

Sometimes, people resist detailed planning because they're used to working more spontaneously or reactively. To change this mindset, communicate the long-term benefits of planning and preparation. Share stories of success where thorough planning led to significant achievements, helping your team see the value in these efforts.

Adapting to a Dynamic Business Environment

Static plans can quickly become outdated. Adopt a mindset of continuous improvement and agility. Regularly review and update your plans based on new information, trends, and advancements. Use scenario planning to prepare for different outcomes, ensuring your business is flexible enough to pivot when needed. Set up feedback loops within your organisation to keep your plans grounded in real-time insights.

Simplifying Complex Processes

More complex processes can lead to inefficiencies. Involve your team in simplifying workflows—they often have the best insights into what's working and what's not. Consider training on Lean or Six Sigma methodologies to empower employees with the tools to streamline processes and boost overall efficiency.

Balancing Short-Term and Long-Term Goals

It's easy to get caught up in day-to-day operations, but keeping your long-term goals in sight is essential. Regular strategic reviews can help ensure your short-term plans are aligned with the bigger picture. Allocate the right resources—time, personnel, and budget—to support immediate needs and future growth.

Managing Stakeholder Expectations

Be transparent with stakeholders about the benefits of structured planning and processes. Clear communication helps manage expectations and builds buy-in, especially when stakeholders resist change. Involve key players in planning to ensure your strategies are realistic and achievable. Keep them updated regularly so they stay engaged throughout the implementation phase.

YOUR ROUTE TO SUCCESS

Building a successful business starts with precise, strategic planning. Focusing on planning, preparation, and efficient processes will set your organisation up for long-term growth and resilience. From setting actionable goals to managing risks, these elements will guide you through challenges and opportunities, helping you create a thriving, scalable business.

Strategic Planning

Start by setting clear, measurable goals for your business. Develop a comprehensive business plan that includes your vision, mission, market analysis, financial projections, and operational strategies. This serves as your roadmap, guiding day-to-day operations and helping secure funding if needed. Thorough market research is also crucial—it enables you to understand your industry, target audience, and competition. Include detailed financial forecasts and operational processes to ensure your business runs efficiently, from supply chain management to quality control.

Preparation Techniques

Preparation is vital in navigating uncertainty. Tools like SWOT analysis (Strengths, Weaknesses, Opportunities, Threats) can help you identify and prioritise risks. Once pinpointing the most significant threats, develop mitigation strategies and contingency plans. Test these plans regularly through simulations or drills to ensure they're effective when real challenges arise.

Process Mapping

To streamline your operations, start by mapping out your current workflows. Identify bottlenecks and inefficiencies, then implement changes to simplify and automate tasks where possible. Tools like flowcharts and diagrams can help visualise these processes, making it easier to spot areas for improvement. Regularly review and refine your workflows, adopting a continuous improvement mindset to keep things running smoothly. Document essential procedures with Standard Operating Procedures (SOPs) and train your team to ensure consistency and quality across all business functions.

INSIGHTS FROM MY JOURNEY

I've repeatedly seen that growth is permanently restricted if the basics aren't done brilliantly, whether it's an FTSE plc, an early-stage start-up, or a one-person operation. There's a tendency to focus on the exciting parts of the business—innovation, growth strategies, big-picture visions—but without a solid foundation of planning, processes, and preparation, none of that can be sustained.

My most successful clients are those who've realised this hard truth. Many come to me after feeling stuck, realising that they've been hamstrung by not investing in the foundational elements of their business. The turning point often comes when they recognise that by focusing on the unglamorous but essential aspects—such as refining processes, tightening up operations, or putting proper planning structures in place—they can unlock new levels of growth and efficiency.

With my guidance, these clients have transformed their journey. By prioritising the foundational work that many overlook, they've built businesses that are more resilient, agile, and ready to seize new opportunities.

9.TECHNOLOGY TALKS

The pace of technological advancements is astounding, transforming industries across the board. From automation and artificial intelligence (AI) to big data and cloud computing, technology is redefining how companies operate, make decisions, and compete in the market. The excitement and anticipation of these changes are palpable as businesses look forward to the possibilities of new technology.

Think about how technology has revolutionised various aspects of business operations. In logistics, advanced tracking systems and automated warehouses have streamlined supply chains, cutting costs and speeding up delivery times. This means your products reach customers faster, enhancing their experience and boosting your reputation. In marketing, data analytics and machine learning algorithms allow precise targeting and personalisation, driving higher customer engagement and conversion rates. You can better understand your customers, tailoring your messages to meet their needs.

Moreover, collaborative tools like video conferencing and project management software have changed how teams work together. Without geographical barriers, your team can communicate seamlessly, share ideas, and work on projects in real time, regardless of location. This fosters a more dynamic and cohesive work environment where creativity and productivity thrive.

LEADING THE WAY

Over the past decade, artificial intelligence (AI) has emerged as one of the most transformative technologies, revolutionising how businesses operate and engage with customers and employees. AI is not just a tool for efficiency; it's allowing companies to automate mundane tasks, freeing up time for more creative, strategic work. AI presents a tremendous opportunity for forward-thinking leaders to drive innovation, enhance productivity, and create a more exciting, dynamic environment for teams and customers. This transformative power of AI inspires and motivates business leaders to embrace it.

The Rise of AI: Automating the Mundane

AI has quickly moved from a futuristic concept to a practical, everyday tool that businesses of all sizes can leverage. From chatbots and virtual assistants to machine learning algorithms that predict customer behaviour, AI is helping companies automate time-consuming, repetitive tasks, enabling employees to focus on more value-added activities. This practicality reassures business leaders, making them feel confident in applying AI.

For example, AI-powered systems can handle routine customer service enquiries, leaving your support teams free to tackle more complex and meaningful customer interactions. Automated data entry, invoicing, and scheduling save hours of manual work, reducing the risk of errors and improving operational efficiency. This automation boosts productivity and allows employees to focus on solving problems, being creative, and delivering exceptional customer value.

AI and Customer Experience: Creating Personalised Connections

AI doesn't just make internal processes more efficient; it also significantly enhances the customer experience. With AI, businesses can offer personalised experiences at scale, tailoring product recommendations, marketing messages, and customer interactions based on individual preferences and behaviours. AI algorithms analyse customer data to predict needs, personalise offers, and improve engagement.

Imagine an online retail business that uses AI to suggest products to customers based on their previous purchases, search history, and even the time of year. This personalisation makes the customer feel understood and valued, which drives higher engagement and loyalty. For your business, AI can be a powerful tool for building stronger relationships with your customers by offering them precisely what they want when they need it most.

Exciting Your Team: AI as a Catalyst for Innovation

Far from replacing human roles, AI serves as a catalyst for innovation within teams. By automating unsexy tasks—like data processing or repetitive administrative work—AI frees employees to focus on higher-level strategic thinking, creative projects, and problem-solving. This shift from mundane to meaningful work enhances job satisfaction, making teams more engaged and motivated.

AI-powered tools like project management software, intelligent document processing, and workflow automation allow employees to work more efficiently and collaborate more effectively. These tools take the burden of routine tasks off their shoulders, allowing them to focus on driving the business forward with new ideas and solutions. When freed from repetitive tasks, employees can contribute to a continuous improvement and innovation culture, helping your business stay ahead of the competition.

The development of AI has opened new doors for businesses, enabling them to automate their routines while exciting teams and customers alike. By embracing AI, you can streamline your operations, enhance customer experience, and empower your employees to focus on what matters—creativity, problem-solving, and innovation.

NAVIGATING THE WHY

When you integrate technology into your business operations, you base your decisions on solid scientific principles that enhance organisational performance and resilience. Understanding the science behind these advancements enables you to make more informed choices about technology adoption and implementation.

Digital Transformation

Digital transformation can revolutionise business processes through automation, artificial intelligence (AI), and machine learning (ML). Automation helps streamline operations, reducing manual tasks and boosting efficiency. AI and ML can analyse vast amounts of data to provide insights that drive strategic decisions. For example, e-commerce platforms use AI to recommend products based on user behaviour, while customer relationship management (CRM) systems track interactions to improve service.

Efficiency Gains

Research consistently shows that businesses adopting technology see significant improvements in efficiency and productivity. Robotic process automation (RPA) can handle repetitive tasks such as data entry, invoicing, and customer service enquiries, freeing your employees to focus on more exciting activities. AI tools truly shine in data analysis, more efficiently and accurately uncovering patterns and trends that inform your business strategies. For example, predictive analytics can forecast sales trends, helping you optimise inventory and marketing efforts.

Psychological Impact

Technology plays a crucial role in reducing cognitive load and enhancing productivity. Project management tools, in particular, are instrumental in helping you and your team stay organised, set deadlines, and allocate resources efficiently. These tools streamline workflows, reducing the mental burden on your team and allowing them to focus on their tasks. Digital tools, particularly those that help maintain focus and organisation, contribute to better time management and task completion rates. For instance, calendar apps and scheduling software ensure deadlines are met and conflicts are avoided. Access to advanced tools and resources fosters a culture of innovation. Technologies like 3D printing and virtual reality (VR) enable rapid prototyping and testing, accelerating the development of new products and solutions. Collaborative software and virtual whiteboards allow your teams to brainstorm and experiment with ideas in real-time, promoting creative problem-solving.

Neuroscience of Technology

Studies in neuroscience show that using technology effectively can enhance cognitive functions such as memory, attention, and problem-solving. Digital tools that assist with data visualisation help you better understand complex information and make informed decisions. Tools like Microsoft's *Power BI* and *Tableau* provide interactive data visualisation, allowing you to see trends and insights, leading to better decision-making. Automating routine tasks reduces stress by minimising the mental load on employees, enabling them to focus on engaging and meaningful work, increasing job satisfaction and reducing turnover rates. Technologies that support remote work and flexible schedules contribute to a healthier work-life balance, reducing burnout and improving overall wellbeing.

By understanding the scientific principles behind technological advancements, you can better appreciate these tools' profound impact on efficiency, productivity, and innovation. Leveraging these insights allows you to make strategic decisions that harness technology's full potential, driving your organisation toward tremendous success and sustainability. This sense of achievement can be a powerful motivator for you and your team.

IT'S NOT ALL PLAIN SAILING

Introducing new technology into your business is a journey filled with opportunities and challenges. Knowing the potential hurdles and planning for them is essential for a smooth transition and lasting success.

Fear of the Unknown

It's natural for employees to feel uncertain or resistant when new technology is introduced. The disruption to established routines can create anxiety. To ease these concerns, communicate the benefits clearly—show how the technology will simplify their work, improve efficiency, and contribute to the company's overall success.

Develop a robust change management plan that includes training sessions, open forums for discussion, and ongoing support throughout the transition. Highlight quick wins and success stories to build confidence in the new system. Involve employees by asking for their input and addressing their concerns. Form committees with team members from different departments to ensure everyone feels heard and engaged.

Implementation Costs

Adopting new technology often comes with a significant upfront cost. Beyond purchasing software or hardware, there's training, potential downtime, and ongoing maintenance to consider. Careful budgeting is critical—plan for the initial investment and long-term expenses like upgrades and continued training.

While the initial cost may seem high, focus on the long-term return on investment (ROI). Think about how the technology will save money by boosting efficiency, reducing errors, and improving productivity. To ease the financial burden, explore options like financing, leasing, or payment plans offered by vendors. See grants or incentives available through government programs or industry associations to support tech adoption.

Data Security and Privacy

Protecting your company's data is a top priority, especially when adopting new technologies. Ensure you have robust security measures, such as data encryption (both in transit and at rest), strict access controls, and regular security audits. Encryption safeguards sensitive data from unauthorised access, while multi-factor authentication and role-based permissions ensure that only the right people can access critical information.

Conduct regular security audits to identify any vulnerabilities and address them promptly. It's also vital to have an incident response plan ready in case of a data breach, with clear steps for containing the breach, notifying affected parties, and restoring systems quickly.

Compliance

Staying compliant with data protection regulations is a must. Regulations like GDPR in Europe or CCPA in the US set specific guidelines for how businesses handle personal data. Ensure your business is fully compliant by maintaining accurate records, obtaining consent, and giving customers control over their data.

Review your compliance measures regularly and update them as legislation evolves. This includes conducting internal audits, training employees on compliance requirements, and staying informed about regulatory changes. Develop a strong data governance policy that outlines how data is collected, stored, and protected, and keep it updated to ensure you meet all legal obligations.

Maintaining Technological Relevance

Technology evolves rapidly, and keeping up can be challenging. Systems can become outdated quickly, so staying informed about new advancements in your industry is essential. Monitor tech trends and innovations that could benefit your business regularly.

Encourage a culture of adaptability within your organisation, where teams are open to experimenting with new tools and technologies. Building solid relationships with technology vendors and consultants can also help. They can provide insights into emerging trends and support your team with training and implementation.

YOUR ROUTE TO SUCCESS

Success lies in adopting the latest tools and aligning them with your business's unique goals and challenges. Whether you're selecting the right technologies, planning their implementation, or upskilling your team, every step requires thoughtful decision-making and adaptability. By embracing a clear, well-structured approach to technology, you can drive efficiency, foster innovation, and future-proof your business.

Identifying the Right Technologies

Start by assessing your business's needs and challenges. Talk to different departments to understand their specific requirements—your marketing team might need advanced analytics, while operations could benefit from automation.

Choose technologies that solve current problems and can scale as your business grows. Opt for solutions that integrate seamlessly with your existing systems and support your long-term goals. Prioritise user-friendly tools that your team can adopt quickly—complex systems often lead to frustration and low usage.

Research and Selection

When evaluating technology options, compare features, costs, and benefits across multiple solutions. Create a decision matrix to weigh critical factors like functionality, ease of use, scalability, and vendor reputation.

Engage with vendors directly to get demonstrations, trial periods, and case studies that show how their solutions have worked for similar businesses. Stay informed by attending industry conferences, webinars, and trade shows, and network with other business leaders and tech experts to get insights and recommendations.

Implementation Plan

Develop a detailed plan for rolling out the new technology. Outline the steps, set timelines, define budgets, and assign responsibilities. A phased approach often works best—deploying the technology in one department before expanding it across the business.

Involve key stakeholders in planning to ensure the implementation addresses everyone's needs and concerns. Communicate progress regularly, gather feedback, and make adjustments as needed. Pilot programs are a great way to test the waters before a full-scale rollout. They allow you to identify issues and gather feedback early, helping you refine the technology and your implementation strategy.

Training and Upskilling

Offer comprehensive training programs to ensure your team is equipped to use the new technology. Mix workshops, online courses, and hands-on sessions to cater to different learning styles. Tailor training to specific roles and departments so that it's relevant and practical.

Encourage a culture of continuous learning, where employees stay updated with new tech advancements and best practices. Foster knowledge-sharing within the organisation through team meetings, internal webinars, or knowledge-sharing platforms.

Change Management

Introducing new technology isn't just about the tools—it's about managing the people side of change. Develop a change management plan that addresses potential resistance and communicates the benefits of the new technology. Leaders should actively model the use of the latest systems and keep communication clear and consistent.

Set measurable goals to track the success of your implementation. Monitor productivity improvements, cost savings, adoption rates, and customer satisfaction. Regularly review these KPIs and gather feedback to fine-tune your approach, making data-driven decisions to maximise the impact of your tech strategy.

INSIGHTS FROM MY JOURNEY

Technology has been a game-changer in my business, and I've realised it underpins everything we've covered in this book. Whether creating efficient processes, improving communication, or staying organised, the right tech solutions can transform your work.

Throughout my business journey, I've adopted technology to automate mundane, repetitive tasks that can consume valuable time. By doing so, I've shifted my focus away from administrative work and concentrated on what matters—adding value to my clients. This has made my business more efficient and allowed me to deliver a higher level of service.

Technology has empowered me to create more space for strategic thinking, innovation, and personal connection with clients. It's allowed me to proactively grow my business and create an environment where my clients and I can thrive. I truly believe embracing technology is essential for any business that wants to stay competitive and relevant in the modern world.

SECTION TWO

THE EXPLORER'S TOOLKIT

10. EMBRACE YOUR IMPOSTER

Have you ever questioned your accomplishments, feeling like a fraud despite apparent successes? You're not alone. Many high-achieving professionals experience these doubts, a phenomenon known as Imposter Syndrome. That nagging inner voice tells you that, despite your achievements, you're not as competent as others believe. This internal struggle affected countless individuals, including myself, when I started my own business. Even with evidence of success, the feeling of being undeserving or inadequate can persist, making it hard to embrace your achievements fully.

Common signs of Imposter Syndrome include:

- **Persistent self-doubt:** You question your competence and skills despite your accomplishments.
- **Attributing success to external factors:** You credit luck or timing rather than your ability.
- **Fear of not meeting expectations:** Worrying about failing to meet your or others' expectations.
- **Downplaying success:** You brush off accolades or achievements as *"nothing big"* or *"just part of the job."*

This is a common barrier to personal and professional growth, but it can be overcome with awareness and the right strategies.

LEADING THE WAY

Dame Jessica Ennis-Hill is a shining example of how even the most accomplished individuals struggle with Imposter Syndrome. As a celebrated British heptathlete and Olympic gold medallist, Ennis-Hill's name is synonymous with excellence in athletics. However, despite her extraordinary achievements, including her unforgettable victory at the 2012 London Olympics, Ennis-Hill has openly discussed her struggles with self-doubt and feelings of inadequacy throughout her career.

Overcoming the Imposter Within

Ennis-Hill frequently questioned her abilities throughout her athletic journey, fearing that her success was due to luck or external factors rather than her hard work and talent. Despite being at the pinnacle of her sport, she experienced the persistent internal voice that many of us recognise—the voice that whispers, *"You're not good enough"* or *"Soon, they'll find out you don't belong."*

Ennis-Hill's ability to perform under immense pressure while managing these internal battles is a testament to her incredible mental resilience. Competing in a prominent arena where expectations were sky-high, she had to confront her fears of not living up to other's perceptions of her. Yet, despite these feelings, she delivered an exceptional performance at the 2012 Olympics, proving to the world—and perhaps most importantly to herself—that she deserved her success. Her courage in facing these internal struggles is a source of inspiration for us all.

A Symbol of Mental Strength

What makes Ennis-Hill's story so inspiring is her willingness to share her experience with Imposter Syndrome openly. She has spoken about how she continued to wrestle with self-doubt even after winning an Olympic gold medal and receiving widespread recognition. Her honesty humanises the experience of feeling like an imposter, reminding us that even those who seem to have it all together may still struggle internally. Her openness encourages us to share our own experiences and seek the support we need.

Jessica Ennis-Hill's story is a powerful reminder that Imposter Syndrome can affect anyone, regardless of their success, whether in business or sports. High achievers across all fields experience self-doubt, but her journey shows that the key to overcoming it isn't eliminating those feelings—acknowledging them and pushing them forward despite the doubt. Ennis-Hill teaches us that overcoming Imposter Syndrome means accepting these feelings as a natural part of high achievement. She defined her success by embracing the pressure, managing her fears, and letting her hard work speak for itself.

NAVIGATING THE WHY

We've already learned that Imposter Syndrome is a feeling of inadequacy and a complex psychological phenomenon. It often manifests as a persistent belief in one's incompetence despite evident success and is accompanied by a fear of being exposed as a fraud. This syndrome affects individuals across various professions and levels of achievement, showing that its roots are deeply embedded in our psyche.

Cognitive Foundations

Imposter Syndrome is rooted in a distorted self-assessment—specifically, how one perceives and values achievements. Cognitive psychologists suggest this syndrome is linked to specific thought patterns known as cognitive distortions.

Key among these is:

- **Perfectionism:** Setting excessively high and often unattainable standards for yourself and viewing failure to meet these standards as a sign of personal incompetence or failure.
- **Overgeneralisation:** Viewing a tiny mistake as a failure and evidence of incompetence.
- **Attribution Errors:** Believing successes are due to external factors like luck, while failures are due to personal inadequacy.

Neurological Insights

Neuroscientific research has started to explore how brain activity correlates with feelings of Imposter Syndrome. Studies indicate that heightened activity in areas associated with memory retrieval and emotional regulation might exacerbate feelings of anxiety and fear of failure. These emotional responses can reinforce imposter feelings, creating a cycle of self-doubt and fear.

Social and Environmental Influences

Social psychologists point to the role of upbringing and early educational experiences in shaping one's susceptibility to Imposter Syndrome. For instance, children praised for their innate qualities rather than their efforts might grow up feeling undue pressure to succeed without appearing to struggle. Additionally, environments that emphasise competition and comparison, such as some academic or professional settings, can intensify feelings of being an imposter.

Biological Factors

Certain biological factors may predispose individuals to experience Imposter Syndrome. Hormonal imbalances that affect mood and self-esteem, as well as genetic predispositions to anxiety and depression, can make some individuals more susceptible to imposter feelings.

Psychological Impact

The psychological impact of Imposter Syndrome can be profound. It can lead to a cycle of anxiety, stress, and decreased job satisfaction, which can hinder professional advancement and personal happiness. Understanding these dynamics is crucial for developing effective strategies to combat Imposter Syndrome.

IT'S NOT ALL PLAIN SAILING

Addressing and managing Imposter Syndrome in the workplace comes with its own set of challenges. Recognising and developing strategies to overcome these obstacles is essential to ensure a supportive and productive environment.

Recognising and Admitting Imposter Feelings

One of the biggest challenges is acknowledging and admitting to Imposter Syndrome. You might fear that expressing your self-doubt might be perceived as a sign of weakness or incompetence. This fear can prevent you from seeking help or discussing your feelings with others. Creating a culture where vulnerability is accepted and encouraged is crucial in overcoming this barrier.

Balancing Self-Doubt and Confidence

Finding the right balance between healthy self-doubt and confidence can be difficult. While a certain level of self-doubt can drive you to strive for improvement, excessive self-doubt can lead to paralysis and inaction. As a leader, you must help your team navigate this balance by providing constructive feedback, recognising achievements, and encouraging a growth mindset.

Overcoming Perfectionism

Imposter Syndrome is often linked to perfectionism, in which you set unrealistically high standards for yourself and view any failure to meet these standards as a sign of personal incompetence. Overcoming perfectionism involves redefining success and failure, emphasising the value of learning from mistakes, and celebrating progress rather than perfection.

Creating an Inclusive Environment

An inclusive work environment that values diverse perspectives and experiences can help mitigate feelings of being an outsider or imposter. As a leader, you must create an inclusive culture where everyone feels valued and supported. This includes addressing any biases or stereotypes that may contribute to Imposter Syndrome, particularly for women and minority groups.

Providing Support and Resources

Providing access to resources such as mentorship programs, counselling services, and professional development opportunities can help you manage Imposter Syndrome. Ensure your team members have the support they need to build confidence and overcome self-doubt.

YOUR ROUTE TO SUCCESS

The environment you work and live in can significantly influence your susceptibility to Imposter Syndrome. When you're in a culture that emphasises perfectionism and constant comparison, your feelings of inadequacy can skyrocket. Conversely, environments that foster learning celebrate progress over perfection, and recognising effort can help you mitigate these feelings.

As a leader, you are crucial in shaping a supportive culture that encourages open dialogue about challenges and vulnerabilities. Your role is instrumental in helping employees understand that they're not alone in their feelings and that seeking help is a strength, not a weakness. This empowerment can significantly contribute to mitigating Imposter Syndrome in the workplace.

Imposter Syndrome does not discriminate, affecting individuals across all genders, ages, and cultural backgrounds, yet its impact can vary significantly. For instance, women and minority groups may experience Imposter Syndrome more intensely due to societal stereotypes and biases.

Embracing Imposter Syndrome

Often painted negatively, Imposter Syndrome is something you may try to overcome or hide from. But what if you reconsider its role in your life and career? With its roots deep in self-doubt and a relentless pursuit of perfection, can it be a powerful driver for your personal development and business innovation?

Fostering a Continuous Learning Mindset

The essence of feeling like an imposter is the belief that you have more to learn, a notion that can ignite an unyielding quest for knowledge. This mindset propels you to dive deeper into your field, encouraging continuous education and skill acquisition. In a business context, this means staying ahead of the curve and embracing new technologies and methodologies to drive growth and competitiveness.

Enhancing Empathy and Leadership Skills

As a leader who has experienced Imposter Syndrome, you may find yourself more attuned to your team members' doubts and insecurities. This empathy can foster a more supportive, understanding leadership style, where open discussions about challenges, fears, and personal growth are encouraged. By creating an environment where vulnerability is not seen as a weakness, you can cultivate more robust, cohesive teams.

Driving Innovation Through Self-Reflection

The introspection that comes with Imposter Syndrome can be a powerful tool for innovation. Questioning your knowledge and capabilities can lead to a critical assessment of existing processes, products, and strategies, encouraging a culture of improvement and innovation. This relentless pursuit of betterment, rooted in what some may see as a weakness, can be the spark that leads to breakthrough ideas and transformative change.

Building Resilience and Adaptability

Navigating the challenges of Imposter Syndrome requires resilience—learning to bounce back from setbacks and persist despite feelings of self-doubt. This resilience is invaluable in the fast-paced business world, where adaptability and the ability to withstand pressure are critical to long-term success. By embracing your inner imposter, you're not just overcoming fears but building the mental toughness needed to tackle the inevitable challenges of your career and life.

INSIGHTS FROM MY JOURNEY

Throughout my career, I've been fortunate to step into new roles and take on challenges that pushed me forward. Early on, whenever I moved into a new position, I would feel the familiar pangs of Imposter Syndrome. Back then, I viewed it as a negative—a sign that I wasn't ready or didn't belong in that new role. It constantly reminded me that I was somehow inadequate or out of place.

However, as time passed, I saw Imposter Syndrome differently. I realised that those feelings of self-doubt weren't indicators of failure—they were signs that I was stretching myself, stepping outside my comfort zone, and growing. Now, when I feel that inner imposter creeping in, I don't see it as a weakness. Instead, I recognise it as proof that I'm challenging myself in ways that matter.

Starting my own business was one of the most significant moments where this shift in perspective indeed paid off. The doubt was there, but I embraced it as part of the journey instead of letting it hold me back. That imposter feeling became a source of motivation, driving me to constantly learn, improve, and prove to myself that I was up to the challenge. By flipping the script on Imposter Syndrome, I've seen it as a mirror reflecting my fears and my potential for growth and success.

11. OPEN YOUR MIND

At this moment, life has never been more relentless, so the ability to adapt and grow is more crucial than ever. This adaptability stems from what is known as a Growth Mindset—a concept introduced by psychologist Carol Dweck. A Growth Mindset is the belief that our abilities can be developed through dedication and hard work. Unlike a fixed mindset, which assumes our traits are static and unchangeable, a Growth Mindset thrives on challenges and views failure not as a sign of incompetence but as a springboard for growth and improvement.

LEADING THE WAY

Serena Williams is a shining example of how a Growth Mindset can propel someone to greatness, even in adversity. As one of history's most decorated tennis players, Williams' name is synonymous with resilience, determination, and sports excellence. Her career spanned over two decades and has been marked by numerous challenges—injuries, personal setbacks, and intense competition—yet she defied expectations and pushed the boundaries of what's possible.

Relentless Pursuit of Excellence

Throughout her illustrious career, Williams has faced setbacks that would have ended the journey for many athletes. But instead of being discouraged, she has consistently embraced these challenges as opportunities for growth. Whether refining her technique, improving her mental toughness, or returning stronger after injuries, Williams embodies the essence of the Growth Mindset—viewing every obstacle as a chance to learn and improve.

Her resilience was on full display when she returned to the court after life-threatening complications from childbirth. Despite the challenges of balancing motherhood with professional tennis, she remained committed to self-improvement, continuing to evolve her game and proving that hard work and dedication can keep you at the top, no matter the odds.

A Symbol of Unyielding Determination

What makes Serena Williams' journey so powerful is her ability to embrace failure as part of the process. She is known for meticulously analysing her defeats, learning from them, and using them as fuel to become even better. Her mindset goes beyond tennis—it's a life philosophy that she applies to every aspect of her journey, from her athletic career to her business ventures and philanthropic efforts.

Serena Williams' story serves as a potent reminder that growth comes not from avoiding failure but from embracing it. Her unwavering pursuit of excellence and belief in continuous improvement has kept her at the top of her sport for years. Williams teaches us that success is filled with challenges, setbacks, and a steadfast commitment to personal growth. It's about constantly learning, honing your skills, and persevering through adversity. When faced with obstacles, think of Williams' journey—how she turned failure into motivation and used it as a driving force to keep moving forward.

NAVIGATING THE WHY

Unlocking your potential begins with understanding the profound impact a Growth Mindset can have on your brain. Both neuroscience and psychology offer compelling evidence that our abilities and intelligence are not fixed but can be developed through effort and perseverance. Embracing this mindset can transform challenges into opportunities, boost your resilience, and foster a culture of innovation and adaptability within your team.

Neuroscientific Impact

At the heart of the Growth Mindset is the discovery that the brain is far more malleable than we once believed. Neuroscientific studies show that neurons form new pathways with each new learning experience, and these brain changes enhance our abilities. This concept, known as neuroplasticity, supports the idea that intelligence and talents can be developed through practice and perseverance.

Deep within our brains lies the potential for remarkable transformation. Neuroscience has shown that our brains are not fixed structures but adaptable landscapes that can change throughout our lives. When we learn something new, our brain cells, or neurons, form new connections, and with repeated use, these pathways become more muscular. This science supports the idea that we can improve our abilities with dedication and effort.

Psychological Impact

Psychological studies complement these findings by highlighting how a Growth Mindset influences motivation and achievement. People with a Growth Mindset are more likely to embrace challenges, persist through setbacks, and see effort as a path to mastery. They tend to learn from criticism and find inspiration in others' success. This contrasts sharply with a fixed mindset, where individuals believe their abilities are static and thus avoid challenges, give up quickly, and feel threatened by others' achievements.

Understanding this can be liberating. It means that the capacity to learn and grow is not fixed at birth but is an ongoing possibility. Whether you're learning to code, mastering digital marketing, or navigating leadership complexities, each challenge is not just a test but an opportunity to expand your abilities.

Adopting a Growth Mindset can also foster a more innovative and resilient business culture. Teams with a Growth Mindset are more collaborative, willing to take risks, and better equipped to adapt to changing market conditions. This cultural shift can lead to more creative solutions and a sustained competitive advantage.

IT'S NOT ALL PLAIN SAILING

Adopting a Growth Mindset, while transformative, comes with its challenges. Understanding these pitfalls can enhance your growth journey, turning potential stumbling blocks into stepping stones for success.

Effort vs. Strategic Effort

One common misconception is that mere effort is enough for success. While effort is crucial, it must be purposeful and informed by strategic thinking and reflection. For instance, if a marketing strategy fails to deliver the desired outcomes, merely intensifying efforts without reevaluating tactics is unlikely to yield better results. Recognising this pitfall allows you and your team to work smarter by applying a reflective approach to each task—analysing what worked, what didn't, and why.

The Fixed Mindset in Disguise

Another subtle pitfall is the principle of a fixed mindset in disguise. This occurs when leaders commend effort but fail to provide constructive feedback, resulting in complacency. To turn this pitfall into a growth opportunity, feedback should be specific, actionable, and focused on the process and strategies rather than personal traits. This encourages individuals to think critically about enhancing their skills and approaches, fostering a true Growth Mindset.

Overcoming Resistance to Change

Resistance to change is a natural human response. As a leader, you must be patient and persistent, providing continuous support and encouragement to help your team transition from a fixed to a Growth Mindset. This may involve regular training sessions, workshops, and one-on-one coaching to reinforce the principles and benefits of a Growth Mindset.

Dealing with Setbacks

Setbacks are inevitable, and how you respond to them is crucial. A Growth Mindset encourages viewing setbacks as learning opportunities, but this can be difficult to maintain in the face of repeated failures. Model resilience and a positive attitude toward setbacks, demonstrating that failure is a natural part of the learning process and an opportunity to grow stronger and more capable.

YOUR ROUTE TO SUCCESS

Cultivating a Growth Mindset isn't just about changing your beliefs; it's about embedding them into your daily practices and interactions. For leaders, this transformative process involves a series of intentional steps reinforcing the belief that every challenge is a learning opportunity and every failure is a stepping stone to success.

Self-Awareness and Mindset Recognition

Your journey begins with self-awareness. Listen to your internal dialogue to recognise and acknowledge your mindset. Do you fear failure, avoid challenges, or feel threatened by others' success? These are signs of a fixed mindset. Start shifting these thoughts by framing challenges as opportunities and failures as lessons. When faced with a setback, instead of telling yourself, *"I can't do this,"* ask, *"What can I learn from this experience?"*

Setting Learning Goals

While performance goals drive you to achieve specific results, learning goals focus on what you gain from the process. For instance, if you're working on a new marketing campaign, a performance goal might be to increase engagement by 25%, while a learning goal could be to master a new digital tool or understand consumer behaviour more deeply. This dual focus ensures you extract value and growth from the experience, regardless of the outcome.

Embracing Feedback

Feedback plays a crucial role in developing a Growth Mindset. Actively seek input, not just in formal reviews but in day-to-day interactions. Approach feedback with curiosity rather than defensiveness. This could mean asking clients or colleagues for insights after presentations or meetings and reflecting on what went well and what could be improved. When you receive criticism, reframe it as constructive advice aimed at helping you improve rather than as a personal slight.

Celebrating the Process

Another practical tip is to celebrate the process, not just the outcomes. Recognise the small steps you take each day that contribute to your larger goals. Did you engage with a new networking group? Did you experiment with a new business strategy? Each of these actions is a testament to your commitment to growth. By valuing the process, you build resilience and maintain momentum even when results are not immediately apparent.

Maintaining a Reflective Journal

Documenting your thoughts, feelings, successes, and setbacks helps you to see your progress over time. It also serves as a reflective practice that can deepen your understanding of how you approach problems, handle stress, and adapt to new information. Reviewing this journal can provide a powerful reminder of how far you've come and what you've learned, reinforcing your commitment to a Growth Mindset.

Fostering Team Learning

As a leader, you face the challenge of consistently engaging your teams in learning. This involves creating a culture where setting challenges, learning from outcomes, making necessary adjustments, and trying again become a natural cycle. One effective strategy is to implement regular innovation sessions where team members can propose solutions to existing problems, test new ideas, and learn from successes and failures in a supportive environment. These sessions encourage a hands-on approach to learning and underline the importance of persistence and flexibility.

Structured Reflection

Cultivating a reflection routine is critical to effectively sustaining a growth mindset. This should be a structured practice where you and your team regularly reflect on your experiences. By examining what worked, what didn't, and how approaches can be improved, setbacks are transformed into opportunities for growth. This reflection deepens understanding and enhances the ability to apply lessons learned to future challenges.

Integrating Feedback Mechanisms

Integrating reflective practices with formal feedback mechanisms can further solidify a Growth Mindset. Encouraging team members to give and receive constructive feedback fosters open communication and promotes mutual learning. As a leader, facilitate this process by modelling how to provide balanced feedback that acknowledges efforts and suggests actionable steps for improvement. This helps build a supportive workplace where continuous learning is part of everyone's role.

INSIGHTS FROM MY JOURNEY

Towards the end of my corporate career, I made a decision that, at the time, felt unconventional—I moved from a corporate support role in Finance into Hospitality Operations. It wasn't a typical career move, as few people shifted from the back office to the front lines of the business. But it was a clear example of a Growth Mindset in action for me.

I was driven to learn more and experience a different business side. I knew that stepping into Operations would give me a deeper understanding of how the business worked and expand my skillset in ways that would be valuable for the future. It was a challenge, but my curiosity and commitment to continuous learning have always pushed me forward.

This decision paid off regarding personal growth and the insights I could bring when working with others. By staying open to new experiences and not limiting myself to a single path, I've been able to continually learn and adapt, which has helped me help others. That's the essence of a Growth Mindset—embracing the opportunities of stepping into the unknown.

12. UNDERSTAND YOUR IMPACT

Imagine embarking on a journey that takes you deep into your emotions, strengths, weaknesses, and motivations. This journey of self-awareness is a fundamental aspect of effective leadership, enabling you to make more informed decisions, navigate interactions with greater skill, and foster personal growth.

In many cultures, self-awareness is closely tied to wisdom and ethical behaviour. For leaders, this translates into thoughtful and moral decision-making. You become more conscious of your impact on others, leading with integrity and inspiring your team through your actions. By understanding yourself better, you develop a heightened sensitivity to the needs and emotions of those around you, cultivating a workplace rooted in trust, respect, and collaboration.

As you enhance your self-awareness, you also strengthen your ability to reflect on your choices and actions. This reflective practice helps you learn from experience, adapt strategies, and approach challenges more rationally. Leading with self-awareness grounds your leadership in empathy and ethics, setting a solid example for your team and creating a ripple effect that elevates your organisation's culture and effectiveness.

LEADING THE WAY

Melanie Perkins, co-founder and CEO of Canva, exemplifies the power of self-awareness in leadership. At 36, she has transformed a startup into a multi-billion-dollar company while maintaining a strong sense of purpose and humility. Perkins' success is rooted in her ability to understand herself, recognise her strengths and limitations, and lead with emotional intelligence.

The Power of Conscious Leadership

From the outset, Perkins knew she didn't have all the answers. Rather than letting this hold her back, she embraced her limitations and sought help from mentors and experienced professionals. This self-awareness allowed her to make strategic decisions for Canva, relying on the expertise of others to fill gaps in her knowledge and ensuring that her ego never got in the way of building a robust and collaborative team.

Her leadership style is characterised by emotional intelligence and humility. Perkins has spoken openly about the importance of recognising when to step back and let others take the lead in areas where they have more experience. This self-awareness has fostered a culture of openness and feedback at Canva, where employees feel empowered to contribute and grow.

A Symbol of Reflective Leadership

What sets Perkins apart is her deep understanding of how her actions and decisions impact those around her. She recognises that leadership is not about being the loudest voice in the room but about listening, learning, and adapting. This awareness has helped Canva grow while staying true to its core values of inclusivity, transparency, and creativity.

Melanie Perkins' story powerfully reminds leaders and aspiring entrepreneurs that self-awareness is essential to success.

Understanding when to seek help, embracing feedback, and being mindful of your leadership style can foster a culture of growth, innovation, and collaboration.

Perkins' journey shows that leadership isn't about knowing everything; it's about understanding yourself and those you lead. It's about recognising when to step back, relying on others' strengths, and creating an environment where everyone feels valued and empowered to contribute.

NAVIGATING THE WHY

Psychological research and neuroscience lay a solid foundation for the importance of self-awareness. Studies suggest that self-aware individuals enjoy better mental health, stronger relationships, and more effective leadership.

The Neurological Impact

Let's explore how our brains affect self-awareness. Certain parts of the brain, like the anterior cingulate cortex (ACC) and the medial prefrontal cortex (mPFC), help us understand ourselves better. These areas allow us to process information about ourselves, and understanding how they work can improve our leadership skills and business decision-making.

The ACC helps you spot mistakes, anticipate tasks, and stay motivated. When you make a wrong move or face a challenge, this part of the brain assesses the situation and signals when to make changes. In business, this is essential because you constantly have to evaluate decisions and adjust your strategies. When you're in tune with this, you better recognise and fix mistakes, leading to more effective and polished business practices.

The mPFC, on the other hand, is all about self-reflection and understanding emotions—yours and others. It helps you think about your actions, understand how people see you, and make decisions considering your team's emotions and dynamics. This ability to reflect on yourself and empathise with others is vital to being a strong leader, as it helps you navigate tricky interpersonal situations and build a positive work environment.

The Psychological Impact

Beyond neuroscience, psychological research into self-awareness significantly influences various aspects of organisational behaviour. A self-aware leader is typically better at managing workplace conflicts, guiding your team through challenges, and communicating effectively. You can identify your strengths and weaknesses, allowing you to delegate tasks more effectively and harness the strengths of others to compensate for your limitations. Studies also link self-awareness to emotional intelligence, a critical factor in leadership effectiveness. Leaders with high emotional intelligence and self-awareness can better manage their emotions and those of others, improving workplace relationships and increasing overall morale. This emotional regulation is essential for maintaining a stable and positive work environment.

Self-aware leaders are more adaptable and flexible, crucial traits for navigating the complexities of modern business environments. By understanding your cognitive and emotional biases, you can make more objective and balanced decisions, mitigating risks associated with biased decision-making. This self-knowledge leads to more rational and effective strategies. Recognising your limitations can lead to a more collaborative approach where ideas are freely shared and valued. This openness to innovation and collaboration drives continuous improvement and maintains a competitive edge for you and your entire organisation.

Transparency and honesty about your strengths and limitations can foster trust within your team. Being open about your learning process can inspire others to engage in their professional development, creating a culture of continuous improvement. This environment of trust and mutual respect encourages team members to strive for excellence and support one another in their growth, fostering a positive and productive work environment.

IT'S NOT ALL PLAIN SAILING

Developing self-awareness is challenging. You may struggle with cognitive biases, such as confirmation bias, where you seek information that confirms your preconceptions and ignore contradictory evidence. Overcoming these biases requires deliberate practice and a commitment to self-improvement. Practical strategies for enhancing self-awareness include engaging in regular self-reflection, seeking feedback from peers and mentors, and practising mindfulness. These techniques allow you to step back and evaluate your thoughts and behaviours more objectively, leading to greater self-understanding and personal growth.

Overcoming Cognitive Biases

One significant challenge in developing self-awareness is overcoming cognitive biases. Biases such as the *Dunning-Kruger* effect, where you might overestimate your abilities, and confirmation bias can distort self-perception. To combat these biases, seek diverse perspectives and be open to feedback that may challenge your preconceived notions. Engaging in critical thinking exercises and exposing yourself to different viewpoints can help mitigate these biases.

Balancing Self-Awareness and Self-Criticism

Another challenge is balancing self-awareness with self-criticism. While self-awareness involves recognising your weaknesses, excessive self-criticism can reduce self-esteem and confidence. It is essential to approach self-awareness with a growth mindset, viewing weaknesses as opportunities for improvement rather than flaws. Celebrating small victories and progress can help maintain a positive outlook.

Consistency in Practice

Maintaining consistency in self-awareness practices can also be challenging. The demands of daily business operations can make it easy to neglect self-reflection and mindfulness. However, integrating these practices into your routine is vital for sustained self-awareness. Setting aside time for reflection, seeking regular feedback, and incorporating mindfulness exercises into your schedule can help overcome this challenge.

Creating a Supportive Environment

Self-awareness requires a supportive environment where you feel safe expressing vulnerabilities and seeking feedback. As a leader, foster a culture of psychological safety, encouraging your team to share their thoughts and experiences without fear of judgment. This environment can significantly enhance the effectiveness of self-awareness practices and promote collective growth.

YOUR ROUTE TO SUCCESS

Understanding the profound impact of self-awareness can transform your leadership style. You can maintain professional composure and create a positive workplace atmosphere by comprehending and managing your emotions and reactions. This approach encourages open communication and collaborative problem-solving. Recognising the dynamics of your interactions with others can build stronger relationships within your teams and with external stakeholders.

Regular Self-Reflection

Maintain a reflective journal to document your daily interactions, decisions, and feelings. Over time, patterns will emerge that highlight your typical reactions and biases, offering insights into areas for personal growth. This practice helps you track your progress and provides a clear picture of your developmental journey.

Seeking Feedback

Encourage a culture of feedback within your team. Structured feedback sessions can provide critical insights into your leadership effectiveness and reveal areas that may require improvement. Constructive feedback from peers, subordinates, and mentors can help you see blind spots and areas for growth that you might not have noticed on your own.

Mindfulness Practices

Engage in mindfulness exercises to better connect with your present experiences. This practice helps you recognise your mental and emotional states without judgment, enhancing your capacity to manage them effectively. Meditation, deep breathing exercises, and mindful observation can significantly improve self-awareness.

Professional Coaching

Work with a coach who can provide unbiased feedback and help identify blind spots in your self-perception. Coaches use techniques rooted in psychology to challenge your assumptions and broaden your self-awareness. They can offer new perspectives and strategies to enhance your leadership effectiveness.

Biofeedback and Neurofeedback

Utilise technology to gain insights into physiological processes that reflect mental states, helping you become more aware of your stress responses and emotional triggers. These tools can provide real-time feedback on how your body responds to different situations, allowing you to develop better control over your emotional and physiological responses.

INSIGHTS FROM MY JOURNEY

I never fully appreciated the power of self-awareness and its impact on others' success until I completed the *Insights Discovery* profiling exercise. This exercise was a true turning point for me—it opened my eyes to how I interacted with others and why, in certain situations, I would react impulsively rather than responding thoughtfully. I learned that my behaviour patterns weren't just random; they were shaped by my natural preferences and how I processed information and emotions in various contexts.

Understanding these patterns was like being handed the tools to better manage myself, especially in high-pressure or emotionally charged situations. Rather than being swept up by stress or tension, I now knew the importance of pausing, reflecting, and responding in a way aligned with my core values and the outcomes I wanted to achieve. This small but crucial shift in mindset has had a profound effect not only on how I handle challenging situations but also on how I interact with those around me. My relationships and decision-making in business have become more thoughtful, grounded, and practical, allowing me to lead with more clarity, intention, and empathy.

The realisation that my level of self-awareness could directly influence the success of others was compelling. As a leader, every action, reaction, and communication style sets the tone for the people I work with. I created a more positive and productive environment by recognising how my behaviour affected the team—whether through my tone of voice, body language, or how I handled conflict. It wasn't just about being more conscious of myself; it was about understanding the ripple effect of self-awareness on a team's dynamic and overall performance.

13. BETTER WORKING TOGETHER

Where markets are constantly evolving, and technology is advancing rapidly, businesses that embrace a culture of collaboration genuinely thrive. When you harness your team's collective intelligence and diverse perspectives, you unlock groundbreaking ideas and solutions that no one could achieve alone.

Collaboration extends beyond just teamwork within your company. It involves engaging with external stakeholders, clients, and sometimes even competitors. This broader strategy creates a synergy that amplifies the strengths of all involved, leading to increased productivity, efficiency, and agility. For any business leader or entrepreneur, developing solid collaborative skills is essential to navigating the complexities of the modern market and driving sustained success. Building these cooperative connections allows you to turn challenges into opportunities, fuelling innovation and pushing boundaries.

LEADING THE WAY

The story of Deliveroo and its partnerships with local restaurants is a prime example of how collaboration can drive success through innovation and customer-centric solutions. What started as a simple food delivery service has evolved into a disruptive force in the restaurant industry, fundamentally changing how people access their favourite meals.

Revolutionising Food Delivery

Founded in 2013, Deliveroo quickly identified a gap in the market: while major chain restaurants were set up for delivery, many smaller, local eateries were not. Customers wanted more diverse, high-quality food options delivered quickly, and small restaurants lacked the infrastructure to meet that demand.

Recognising this challenge as an opportunity, Deliveroo forged partnerships with independent restaurants, helping them enter the delivery market without needing a fleet of delivery drivers or logistical operations. In return, Deliveroo expanded its offerings, making it easier for customers to enjoy meals from their favourite local spots at home.

But Deliveroo didn't stop there. They innovated further with *Deliveroo Editions*, delivery-only kitchens explicitly designed for restaurants looking to expand their reach without the cost of a physical location. This initiative allowed small businesses to scale and access new customers while providing a broader range of food options for Deliveroo users.

A New Era of Dining

By fostering a mutually beneficial collaboration with local restaurants, Deliveroo has created a system where everyone wins. Restaurants can grow their businesses without significant investment, customers can access a broader array of dining options, and Deliveroo has cemented itself as a leader in the food delivery market.

This collaboration also significantly impacted the restaurant industry, particularly during the pandemic when delivery services became a lifeline for many eateries. Through these partnerships,

Deliveroo helped keep local businesses afloat while simultaneously meeting the changing needs of their customer base.

An Innovation That Benefits All

Deliveroo's partnership model is a prime example of how collaboration can drive innovation and customer satisfaction. By recognising small restaurants' challenges, the company transformed these obstacles into opportunities for mutual success. Deliveroo has redefined the dining experience through collaboration with local eateries, making restaurant-quality meals more accessible to a broader audience.

Deliveroo's journey shows that true collaboration goes beyond simply working together—it's about forming partnerships that innovate and address real-world challenges. By blending the strengths of independent restaurants with a seamless delivery platform, Deliveroo crafted a winning formula that benefits customers, businesses, and the broader market.

NAVIGATING THE WHY

Research in psychology and organisational behaviour consistently shows collaboration leads to better problem-solving, innovation, and resilience. This applies to large teams and individual entrepreneurs who engage with networks of peers, mentors, and industry partners. Collaborative interactions enhance cognitive functions by providing diverse perspectives that challenge individual biases and encourage creative solutions. In the current business landscape, where innovation and agility are key, collaboration becomes an indispensable strategy for maintaining a competitive edge.

Organisational Benefits

When individuals come together, united by a common goal, the collective intelligence of the group amplifies problem-solving, sparks creativity, and builds a stronger, more adaptable organisation. The benefits of fostering a collaborative culture ripple through every layer of the business—from boosting innovation and employee engagement to driving productivity and reducing turnover.

- **Enhanced Problem-Solving:** When diverse minds come together, they bring different perspectives and expertise, leading to more comprehensive and practical solutions. Collaboration fosters a culture of collective intelligence where problems are tackled from multiple angles.

- **Increased Innovation:** Innovation thrives in an environment where ideas can be freely exchanged and built upon. Collaborative teams are more likely to experiment, take risks, and develop groundbreaking ideas. Cross-pollinating ideas within a diverse team can lead to unexpected and valuable innovations.

- **Greater Resilience:** Collaborative organisations are more adaptable and resilient. When challenges arise, teams that work well together can pivot and adjust more effectively. This resilience is crucial in today's business world, where change is constant and often unpredictable.

- **Improved Employee Engagement and Satisfaction:** Collaboration fosters employees' sense of community and belonging. When team members feel that their contributions are valued and that they are part of a supportive network, their job satisfaction and engagement levels increase. This leads to higher productivity and lower turnover rates.

- **Leveraging Collective Strengths:** Collaboration allows businesses to leverage each team member's strengths and talents. By drawing on diverse skills and experiences, organisations can achieve more than they would through individual efforts alone.

Neurological Impact

Recent breakthroughs in neuroscience provide invaluable insights into how brain function shapes collaborative efforts. Research reveals that social interactions deeply influence brain activity, and cooperative environments can enhance cognitive functioning in ways that competitive settings cannot.

For example, functional magnetic resonance imaging (fMRI) studies have shown that when individuals engage in cooperative tasks, there is increased activation in brain regions associated with reward processing. This suggests that collaboration, rather than competition, can trigger positive emotional responses, fostering a more motivated and cohesive team. As leaders, you can leverage this insight by creating work environments that emphasise team success over individual achievements.

Moreover, the synchronisation of brain activity among team members—known as interbrain coherence—has been observed during successful collaborative tasks. This phenomenon enhances mutual understanding and coordination, suggesting that functions requiring tight cooperation should be designed to allow frequent and meaningful interactions among team members. Leaders can structure meetings and projects to encourage dialogue and exchange, improving this neural synchronisation and leading to more effective teamwork.

IT'S NOT ALL PLAIN SAILING

Building a culture of collaboration is a rewarding but often complex journey. It's not without its challenges, and the path to true partnership can be met with resistance, ingrained biases, and inconsistent practices. Yet, overcoming these obstacles is essential for fostering a dynamic, high-performing team. From breaking down cognitive biases to creating an environment where people feel safe to share ideas, the hurdles are real but surmountable. The key lies in understanding these challenges and adopting strategies to address them, ensuring that collaboration becomes a natural and consistent part of your organisation's DNA.

Overcoming Cognitive Biases

Cognitive biases, such as confirmation bias, can hinder effective collaboration. Team members might seek information that confirms their preconceptions and ignore contradictory evidence. To overcome these biases, encourage diverse perspectives and critical thinking. Deliberate practice and a commitment to self-improvement can help mitigate these biases.

Balancing Self-Awareness and Self-Criticism

While self-awareness is crucial for effective collaboration, excessive self-criticism can reduce self-esteem and confidence—approach self-awareness with a growth mindset, viewing weaknesses as opportunities for improvement rather than flaws. Celebrate small victories and progress to maintain a positive outlook.

Consistency in Collaborative Practices

Maintaining consistency in collaborative practices can be challenging amidst the demands of daily business operations. Integrate these practices into your routine for sustained collaboration. Set aside time for team meetings, seek regular feedback, and incorporate collaboration tools into daily workflows to overcome this challenge.

Creating a Supportive Environment

Create a supportive environment where individuals feel safe expressing their vulnerabilities and seeking feedback. Foster a culture of psychological safety, where employees are encouraged to share their thoughts and experiences without fear of judgment. This environment enhances the effectiveness of collaborative practices and promotes collective growth.

Regular Assessment and Adjustment

Maintaining an effective collaborative environment takes time and effort. Regularly assess team dynamics and make necessary adjustments. This might involve revisiting team goals to ensure they align with overall business objectives or reconfiguring teams to optimise collaboration. Continuous improvement is critical to sustaining a collaborative culture.

YOUR ROUTE TO SUCCESS

Fostering a culture of collaboration in your business goes beyond simply encouraging teamwork—it requires a strategic shift in how you build, lead, and maintain your teams. Successful partnership is rooted in intentional practices that break down silos, leverage diverse expertise, and create an environment where innovation and collective problem-solving can thrive.

Building Cross-Functional Teams

Start by forming cross-functional teams to break down silos and encourage information sharing across departments. These teams, composed of members with diverse expertise, can tackle complex problems more creatively and comprehensively. Regular brainstorming sessions can enhance innovation, allowing employees from different backgrounds to contribute ideas and solutions.

Leveraging Modern Tools and Platforms

Use modern tools and platforms to facilitate effective collaboration. Collaborative software enables real-time communication and seamless sharing of resources. These tools ensure your team members are aligned and can collaborate efficiently, regardless of their physical locations. Project management tools help you organise tasks, track progress, and maintain clear communication channels.

Developing a Collaborative Culture

Participate in professional networks, coworking spaces, or online communities to develop a collaborative culture. These platforms offer support and resources that might be inaccessible to you as a business owner. Regular participation in industry workshops and seminars provides valuable networking opportunities that can lead to collaborative projects and partnerships.

Building Strategic Alliances

Focus on building strategic alliances that complement your skill sets and business offerings. Networking events, professional associations, and online communities are vital for creating opportunities for collaboration. Online platforms like LinkedIn can be instrumental in finding and joining relevant groups or initiating discussions that lead to meaningful partnerships.

Embedding Collaborative Practices

Embed collaborative practices in your startup's culture from the outset. Establish open communication channels and encourage an atmosphere where team members feel valued for their contributions, fostering innovation and agility. Regular teambuilding activities and collaborative projects can help instil these practices.

Leadership Development and Mentorship Programs

Enhance collaborative skills among senior team members through leadership development programs that focus on empathy, effective communication, and delegation. Implement mentorship programs where experienced leaders mentor younger employees to enhance knowledge sharing and strengthen your organisational network.

Recognising and Celebrating Collaboration

Acknowledge and celebrate successful collaborations to reinforce the value of these relationships. Small gestures of recognition, such as sharing a collaborator's work on social media or offering reciprocal support, can sustain these business relationships. Regularly acknowledging and rewarding groups for their collaborative efforts reinforces the importance of teamwork and encourages a continuous commitment to collaborative practices.

Maintaining Collaborative Relationships

Sustain a collaborative approach by maintaining and nurturing professional relationships over time. Regularly check in with mentors, schedule periodic meetings with collaborators, and maintain an active presence in professional groups and forums.

INSIGHTS FROM MY JOURNEY

One of the most valuable lessons I've learned is that collaboration doesn't just add value—it multiplies it. You can provide exponentially better client outcomes by working with like-minded people with different experiences. A powerful example of this came from a leadership event I co-created with two business connections. We pooled our collective knowledge and experiences in business and leadership, and the result was far greater than anything we could have achieved individually.

That early collaboration opened up significant opportunities for us as organisers and the businesses and people we worked with. Combining our expertise created a more comprehensive and impactful event that helped leaders grow, adapt, and thrive in their journeys. Collaboration consistently shows me that when you bring diverse strengths together, you increase the value you can offer and foster an environment where innovation thrives.

14. ENDURING THE STORM

Imagine setting sail on a journey where the sea is unpredictable, and the weather can change instantly. That's what running a business often feels like. Recent studies show that only about half of all startups survive beyond five years, and even fewer make it to ten. In such a volatile environment, resilience and adaptability aren't just important to have—they're essential for survival and growth.

With the rapid pace of technological advancements and frequent economic ups and downs, businesses need to be flexible and persistent. Those who weather these storms often become more robust and better prepared to seize new opportunities. Resilience and adaptability help companies to thrive by turning challenges into innovation opportunities.

LEADING THE WAY

Anne Boden, the founder of Starling Bank, is a shining example of resilience and adaptability in the financial services world. In 2014, after leaving a successful career in traditional banking, Boden set out on an ambitious mission to create a bank that would revolutionise how people manage their money. She envisioned a digital-first bank that offered transparency, ease of use, and innovative financial solutions, filling a gap left by high-street banks.

Resilience Through Setbacks

Boden's journey wasn't easy. She faced rejection after rejection from investors and industry insiders, many of whom doubted the viability of a mobile-only bank. Yet, Boden's resilience shone through as she remained committed to her vision, ultimately securing the necessary funding and launching Starling Bank. Her determination in the face of obstacles demonstrates the importance of perseverance and belief in your mission.

Since its launch, Starling Bank has been at the forefront of the fintech revolution, offering innovative services like real-time notifications, fee-free accounts, and seamless international payments. Boden's ability to listen to customer feedback and swiftly implement changes has set Starling apart from its competitors.

Adapting to a Changing Financial Landscape

As the financial landscape continues to evolve, Starling's adaptability has allowed it to grow rapidly and attract a loyal customer base. When the 2020 pandemic hit, Starling Bank's adaptability was tested. Instead of retreating, the bank pivoted quickly, offering government-backed loans to small businesses and introducing tools to help customers manage their finances during uncertain times. Boden's leadership during this period exemplified how resilience and adaptability can help enterprises survive and thrive during crises.

Anne Boden's story reminds us that resilience isn't about avoiding challenges but facing them head-on and adapting to whatever comes your way. Starling Bank's success shows that embracing change, staying flexible, and believing in your vision can turn obstacles into opportunities for growth.

NAVIGATING THE WHY

Why do some people and organisations bounce back from tough times more effectively than others? Research in neuroscience and psychology offers some insights. A key factor is neuroplasticity—the brain's ability to reorganise and form new connections. This adaptability is crucial not only for individuals but also for organisations that encourage learning and mental flexibility. It's a potential for growth and development that offers hope and optimism.

On a psychological level, resilience is closely tied to optimism, a sense of control, and viewing failure as a learning opportunity rather than a setback. Persistence often stems from intrinsic motivation and a passion for long-term goals. Studies show that people with persistence tend to handle frustration better and remain committed to their vision, even in the face of challenges.

Neurological Impact

Think of adaptability in business as the human body's response to change. Our brains are capable of neuroplasticity, which allows them to adapt and form new neural connections. Organisations that encourage a culture of learning and flexibility are better equipped to handle changes. Research has shown that adaptable companies excel in innovation and customer satisfaction, keeping them competitive.

Psychological Considerations

Developing psychological traits that foster adaptability is crucial for personal growth and professional success. These traits help individuals cope with change and empower them to thrive in uncertain environments. Whether cultivating a growth mindset, building emotional resilience, or staying open to new experiences, these psychological attributes are the foundation for becoming more adaptable and resilient in the face of constant change.

- **Growth Mindset:** As you read in chapter 11, a growth mindset encourages embracing challenges, persisting despite setbacks, and learning from criticism—all essential characteristics for developing resilience and adaptability.

- **Emotional Resilience** is the ability to bounce back quickly from adversity or change. Techniques like mindfulness, reflective practice, and cognitive restructuring help build this resilience by enabling individuals to stay calm and manage stress.

- **Openness to Experience:** This trait involves being open to new ideas and unconventional values, which enhances creativity and reduces resistance to change.

IT'S NOT ALL PLAIN SAILING

Building resilience and adaptability within an organisation requires effort and strategy. While the rewards are great, the path is often fraught with challenges. From resistance to change and leadership hurdles to maintaining consistency during transitions, each obstacle presents an opportunity for growth. By addressing these common barriers and implementing practical strategies, you can cultivate a more adaptable and resilient organisation ready to thrive.

Resistance to Change

One significant barrier to adaptability is resistance to change, often rooted in fear of the unknown. Overcoming this requires clear communication about the benefits of change and involving employees early in the process. Provide training and resources to help them understand and embrace new working methods.

Your Role as a Leader

As a leader, you must model adaptability by responding to changes with enthusiasm and strategic focus. You must also show flexibility in your behaviours and decision-making processes, demonstrating that adaptability is valued and rewarded.

Maintaining Consistency

Maintaining quality and service consistency during transitions can be challenging. Implementing a phased approach to change can help manage this balance, allowing teams to adapt incrementally rather than all at once.

Technological Integration

Introducing new technologies can be challenging, requiring changes to existing processes and systems. To ensure they fit well with your business, conduct thorough needs assessments and pilot programs before fully implementing them.

Emotional and Cultural Resistance

Emotional and cultural resistance to change can significantly hinder adaptability efforts. Address these challenges with respectful communication, involve employees in change initiatives, and gradually integrate new practices. Foster an open culture where feedback is encouraged and concerns are promptly addressed.

Building a Supportive Culture

Creating a supportive culture that embraces change is essential for fostering adaptability. Build trust and encourage collaboration across the organisation. Recognise and celebrate small wins, reinforcing the value of adaptability.

Training and Development

Invest in training and development to help employees adapt to new technologies and processes. Offering continuous learning opportunities ensures that your workforce remains skilled and capable of handling changes.

YOUR ROUTE TO SUCCESS

Adapting to change and building resilience are essential skills for thriving in your personal and professional life. In a world that's constantly evolving, your ability to navigate uncertainty, recover from setbacks, and embrace new opportunities will set you apart. These qualities aren't just about bouncing back—they're about growing stronger with each challenge.

Embrace a Growth Mindset

Embracing a growth mindset is critical to building resilience and adaptability. Instead of seeing obstacles as roadblocks, view them as chances to develop new skills and insights. Your abilities and intelligence can evolve through dedication, learning, and perseverance. When confronted with a challenge, rather than saying, *"I can't handle this,"* reframe it by asking, *"What can this teach me?"*

Build Strong Relationships

Strong personal and professional relationships form a robust support network during difficult times. Invest in your relationships by being present, showing empathy, and offering help to others. These connections provide different perspectives and emotional support when you face challenges.

Stay Curious and Open-Minded

Curiosity drives learning and innovation. Stay open to new ideas and experiences and strive to understand different viewpoints. Embracing the unknown and seeking knowledge can lead to unexpected opportunities and solutions.

Develop Problem-Solving Skills

Improve your problem-solving skills by breaking down problems into smaller, manageable parts. Brainstorm potential solutions and evaluate the pros and cons of each option. This systematic approach builds your confidence and adaptability.

Practice Self-Care and Stress Management

Prioritise self-care to build resilience. Maintain a healthy lifestyle with regular exercise, adequate sleep, and a balanced diet. Incorporate mindfulness practises like meditation or yoga to manage stress effectively.

Learn from Setbacks

Treat failures and setbacks as valuable learning opportunities. Reflect on what went wrong, what lessons you can learn, and how you can improve in the future. This approach helps you bounce back more robustly and resiliently.

Set Realistic Goals and Stay Flexible

Set achievable goals but remain flexible. Be prepared to adjust your goals as circumstances change. Flexibility in planning allows you to adapt to unexpected changes while staying focused on your long-term objectives.

Cultivate Optimism

Maintain a positive outlook, even in challenging times. Optimism helps you stay motivated and focused on finding solutions. Practice gratitude and focus on what you can control to build a more positive mindset.

Seek Professional Development

Continuously invest in your personal development. Attend workshops, take courses, and seek mentorship to develop new skills and expand your knowledge. This ongoing learning process enhances your adaptability and resilience.

INSIGHTS FROM MY JOURNEY

In the mid-2000s, I worked for a well-known Midlands-based car manufacturer that went under after years of difficulties. Overnight, around 6,300 employees—including myself—lost their jobs. I had never experienced anything like it. The sudden collapse of a business on that scale was a shock, forcing me to confront uncertainty in ways I hadn't before.

Looking back, I realise this experience was crucial in developing my resilience and adaptability. Facing the aftermath of such a large-scale failure, I had to decide how I would move forward quickly. It wasn't just about survival but finding the inner strength to embrace the unknown and figure out what came next.

What I learned during that time is something I carry with me today: challenges, no matter how daunting, provide crucial learning opportunities. They help shape the mindset that allows you to recognise the solutions you've used in the past and adapt them to future problems.

15. MIND YOUR LANGUAGE

Effective communication goes beyond simply exchanging information; it's about articulating your vision, aligning your team, and fostering strong relationships within your company and with external stakeholders. In today's fast-paced business environment, mastering communication isn't just a valuable skill—it's a critical one for success.

Think of communication as a strategic tool for sharing ideas, emotions, and intentions with empathy and clarity. As a leader, this enables you to inspire others, fuel innovation, resolve problems, and prevent misunderstandings that can lead to conflict or inefficiency. Enhancing your communication skills can significantly strengthen your organisation's performance, resilience, and ability to adapt to challenges.

LEADING THE WAY

WeWork is a striking example of how poor communication can lead to the downfall of even the most promising companies. Once heralded as a groundbreaking startup redefining the modern workspace, WeWork's meteoric rise was followed by a catastrophic fall—mainly due to a mismatch between its vision, internal communication, and financial reality.

Overpromising and Under-Delivering

At the height of its growth, WeWork's leadership communicated an inflated vision of its potential. There were bold declarations that WeWork was not just a real estate company but a tech giant *"changing the world,"* which created unrealistic expectations inside and outside the company. Investors, employees, and customers believed WeWork was a revolutionary force poised for massive global expansion, with little attention paid to the company's precarious financial situation.

This miscommunication of WeWork's actual business model and financial health caused internal confusion. Many employees were swept up in the hype, believing they were part of something far more significant than the reality suggested. However, the company's substantial losses and lack of a clear path to profitability were hidden beneath this grandiose messaging.

The Collapse of Communication

The turning point came in 2019 when WeWork's attempt to go public exposed its shaky finances. The discrepancies between the internal hype and the external reality became glaringly apparent. Reports revealed that the company was bleeding money, and the leadership had failed to communicate a sustainable business model to investors or employees.

The lack of transparency surrounding WeWork's financial instability led to the collapse of its IPO and a massive company restructuring. What had been communicated as a groundbreaking vision was revealed to be more of a marketing façade than a feasible business strategy. The company's financial condition blindsided employees and investors, resulting in mass layoffs, drastic losses, and a tarnished reputation.

A Lesson in Transparency

WeWork's failure is a cautionary tale about the dangers of overpromising and failing to communicate realistically with internal and external stakeholders. The disconnect between the company's vision and its execution led to a loss of trust and confidence from investors and employees.

As your business grows, inspire your team with bold ideas, but keep your communication realistic. It's not just about sharing your vision—it's about setting clear, achievable goals and staying transparent with your employees, investors, and customers.

NAVIGATING THE WHY

Effective communication is a multifaceted challenge. It involves understanding the principles that guide interpersonal interactions, using practical tools to enhance clarity and impact, and navigating the challenges that arise from miscommunication.

The Psychology and Neuroscience

Research in psychology and neuroscience shows that effective communication is about more than words. Non-verbal cues, emotional intelligence, and active listening are all critical components. Studies reveal that our brains are wired to respond to stories and emotional connections, which can make business communications more persuasive and memorable.

Cognitive Load Theory

Cognitive Load Theory suggests that our brains can only handle so much information simultaneously. By understanding and applying this theory, you can design your communication to manage your audience's cognitive load, preventing information overload that can hinder understanding and retention. This is particularly important in business, where decisions must be made quickly and under pressure.

- **Segmentation:** Break down complex information into manageable chunks. This allows the receiver to process each segment fully before moving on to the next, making it easier to understand and remember.
- **Pre-training:** Provide background information or basic concepts beforehand. This prepares the receiver's mind to handle more detailed or complex information during primary communication.
- **Weeding:** Eliminate unnecessary information that does not directly contribute to your message's objective. This focuses the receiver's attention on the most relevant data.
- **Multimedia:** Use diagrams, charts, and other visual aids to support verbal or written communication. Visuals can help clarify complex information and reduce cognitive load.

Mirror Neurons

Mirror neurons are brain cells that respond when we act and see someone else perform the same action. This mirroring behaviour is vital to empathy, as it helps us understand others' actions, intentions, and feelings.

- **Non-verbal Cues:** Be aware of your body language, facial expressions, and tone of voice, as your team members mirror these. Positive non-verbal communication fosters a supportive atmosphere and enhances message reception.
- **Empathy Development:** Engage in behaviours that foster empathetic connections, such as showing genuine concern and attentiveness in interactions.

- **Feedback Sensitivity:** Use mirror neurons to align your delivery with how you want the receiver to feel and react during feedback sessions. This can make feedback more constructive and less aggressive.

Understanding cognitive load and mirror neurons can enhance communication effectiveness and deepen interpersonal connections, leading to more collaborative and productive environments.

Impact on Stakeholder Relationships

Effective communication is crucial for building strong stakeholder relationships. Clear, consistent, and open communication builds trust and transparency, which is essential for maintaining healthy relationships with employees, clients, and partners. For employees, it means understanding the company's vision and their role in it, which enhances engagement and commitment. For clients, clear communication fosters reliability and professionalism, encouraging long-term partnerships.

Moreover, how a company communicates internally and externally reflects its brand identity and values. Companies that communicate authentically and transparently are often viewed favourably, enhancing their market reputation. This attracts quality talent, loyal customers, and interested investors—vital for success.

Economic Benefits

Studies show a direct link between good communication practices and improved business performance. Effective communication boosts employee engagement by ensuring everyone is aligned and motivated towards common goals. Engaged employees are more productive, contribute better to teamwork and innovation, and are less likely to leave, reducing recruitment and training costs.

Transparent and effective communication also leads to higher customer satisfaction. Satisfied customers are more likely to become repeat customers and recommend your business, driving sales and improving the bottom line. Additionally, efficient communication reduces errors and misunderstandings, preventing costly delays and corrective actions, leading to streamlined operations and cost savings.

IT'S NOT ALL PLAIN SAILING

Poor communication can lead to misunderstandings, reduced team cohesion, and missed opportunities. Challenges often arise from cultural differences, assumptions, and emotional reactions. Improving communication requires overcoming entrenched behaviours and resistance to change.

Technological Challenges

While technology facilitates rapid communication, it also introduces challenges. Text-based communication needs nonverbal cues, leading to misunderstandings. More reliance on digital tools can reduce personal interactions that are crucial for building trust.

- **Use Rich Media:** Use video or voice calls instead of emails or messages for complex or sensitive communications. This helps convey tone and intent more clearly.
- **Set Communication Norms:** Establish clear guidelines for how different communication tools should be used. Reserve emails for formal communications and instant messaging for quick check-ins.

- **Regular Meetings:** Schedule in-person or virtual meetings to maintain personal connections and clarify miscommunications.

Inter-generational Communication

Workplaces are becoming more age-diverse, and different generations have different communication styles and preferences.

- **Tailored Communication:** Understand and respect individual preferences. Encourage employees to share their preferred methods of communication.
- **Cross-generational Training:** Implement training programs to help employees understand different generational perspectives and communication styles.
- **Mentoring Programs:** Establish reverse mentoring programs in which younger employees help older colleagues with new technologies and older employees share their experience and wisdom.

YOUR ROUTE TO SUCCESS

Effective communication is a critical skill that benefits individuals across all levels of an organisation. While some people may naturally excel at it, you can develop and refine this skill through practice and training.

Active Listening

Active listening is fundamental to communication. It involves fully concentrating, understanding, responding, and remembering what is said. Practice active listening by summarising the other person's words during a conversation to ensure understanding and show that you are paying attention.

Clarity and Conciseness

Clarity and conciseness are crucial when writing an email or speaking at a meeting. Avoid jargon and overly complicated language. Use simple, direct expressions to ensure your message is understood.

Emotional Intelligence

Understanding and managing your emotions and those of others can significantly enhance your communication effectiveness. Develop emotional intelligence by being aware of non-verbal signals and adjusting your communications accordingly.

Feedback

Giving and receiving feedback effectively is vital. Constructive feedback helps build trust and improve team dynamics. Practice delivering balanced feedback that acknowledges good performance while addressing areas for improvement.

Advanced Technologies

Leverage advanced communication technologies to enhance the clarity and reach of your internal communications:

- **Artificial Intelligence:** Use AI to analyse organisational communication patterns, identify bottlenecks, and improve information flow between departments or levels of the hierarchy.
- **Digital Communication Platforms:** Utilise tools like Slack, Microsoft Teams, and Zoom for real-time communication and collaboration. These platforms integrate video, text, voice communication, and document sharing, supporting remote and distributed teams.

INSIGHTS FROM MY JOURNEY

I've applied what I've learned about effective communication to my own business, especially when working with a wide range of coaching clients. While coaching frameworks are relatively straightforward, the real challenge lies in navigating the conversations. Each client is unique, and understanding how to adjust your communication style to fit the person in front of you can make all the difference in achieving a successful outcome.

I've found that clear and tailored communication helps build trust and openness, allowing clients to feel supported and understood. This principle applies not only to one-on-one coaching but also to business as a whole. The most successful companies I've worked with understand the importance of consistency in their internal and external communication. Whether aligning teams on a common goal or ensuring their messaging to customers is transparent and authentic, businesses that communicate effectively create an environment where everyone feels informed and engaged.

This has been a crucial part of my approach—whether coaching individuals or advising businesses—because I've seen first-hand how powerful communication can be when done correctly. It's not just about what you say but how you say it and ensuring that your message is consistent across all levels of the organisation.

16. YOUR COMPETITIVE EDGE

The ability to wear multiple hats can be your secret weapon. Skill stacking, or combining complementary skills, isn't just about being competent in several areas. It's about blending these abilities to create a unique and marketable set of skills, giving you a distinct advantage in the competitive job market. By integrating multiple skills, you can tackle complex problems, seize new opportunities, and stand out in a business landscape where innovation, agility, and interpersonal dynamics are critical to success.

Understanding and implementing skill stacking can significantly enhance strategic thinking and operational efficiency. This approach allows you to connect different ideas, anticipate market trends, and respond creatively and effectively to industry demands. Skill stacking isn't just about gathering skills randomly; it's about smartly curating a set of abilities that work together to create a compelling value proposition, fostering a culture of innovation and creativity.

LEADING THE WAY

Tim Ferriss is a modern embodiment of the power of skill stacking. Best known as the author of *The 4-Hour Workweek*, Ferriss has built a diverse and influential career by combining a unique mix of skills that might not stand out but create a compelling and rare combination. His journey demonstrates how leveraging multiple complementary skills can lead to extraordinary success.

Mastering the Art of Skill Stacking

Tim Ferriss may not individually be the world's best writer, marketer, or entrepreneur, but what sets him apart is his ability to blend writing, self-experimentation, communication, and business acumen into a unique personal brand. These diverse skills have made him one of the most recognised voices in productivity, self-improvement, and entrepreneurship.

Ferriss's breakthrough book, *The 4-Hour Workweek*, is a perfect example of skill stacking. He didn't just write a book; he used his knowledge of marketing, digital entrepreneurship, and self-experimentation to craft a narrative that resonated with millions. By combining his ability to communicate complex ideas with real-world experiments in lifestyle design, he managed to create a movement, not just a product.

Leveraging Media and Communication

Beyond his books, Ferriss has expanded his influence through his podcast, *The Tim Ferriss Show*, where he applies his storytelling, communication, and networking skills. Ferriss wasn't a professional podcaster when he started, but by combining his deep curiosity, interview skills, and personal branding, he created one of the most popular podcasts in the world. His ability to pull insights from world-class performers across various industries has given him a robust platform that further extends his influence.

The Power of Self-Experimentation

Another critical skill Ferriss stacks is his dedication to self-experimentation. He has developed a reputation for pushing the limits of human performance through biohacking, fitness experiments, and lifestyle optimisations, documenting the results in books like *The 4-Hour Body* and *Tools of Titans*. This unique approach, blending his curiosity with research, self-discipline, and a desire to improve, allows him to offer precious insights to his audience, further reinforcing his brand.

The lesson is clear: Don't focus on mastering one skill alone. Instead, look at how your diverse talents, interests, and experiences can be combined to set you apart from the crowd. By stacking your skills strategically, you'll unlock new opportunities for growth, innovation, and lasting success.

NAVIGATING THE WHY

Engaging in interdisciplinary learning broadens your knowledge and boosts creativity and innovation. This cross-pollination of disciplines encourages a richer exchange of ideas, helping you solve problems more creatively and see connections that might not be apparent when focused on a single field.

Think about how learning both mathematics and music can enhance your cognitive abilities. Each discipline supports abstract thinking, pattern recognition, and skills transferable to various problem-solving areas. Today's innovation often happens at the intersection of disciplines. For example, combining psychology and computer science has led to user-centric software design, significantly enhancing user engagement and satisfaction.

Neuroplasticity

Your brain's ability to form new neural connections, known as neuroplasticity, remains active throughout life. This means you can continually adapt and learn new skills, contrary to the old belief that this ability diminishes significantly with age.

Adult neuroplasticity is supported by neuronal growth, synaptic pruning (where the brain eliminates weaker synaptic connections), and neurogenesis (creating new neurons). These processes are stimulated by mental activity and are crucial for learning new skills and information.

Engaging in new and complex activities enhances neuroplasticity. Think about learning a new language, playing a musical instrument, or engaging in new sports. These activities keep your brain malleable and more capable of integrating new information and skills.

Consider a continuous learning and skill development journey that reshapes your brain, making it more adept at handling further learning and complexity. This proactive approach to personal and professional growth uses ongoing education as both a tool and a lifestyle, keeping your brain healthy and adaptable.

IT'S NOT ALL PLAIN SAILING

Skill stacking offers significant advantages but also comes with its own set of challenges. Juggling multiple commitments, managing time effectively, and overcoming internal doubts can sometimes feel overwhelming. Success lies in navigating these obstacles with practical strategies and the right mindset. Whether mastering time management or tackling psychological barriers like imposter syndrome, understanding how to manage these challenges will keep you on track and motivated.

Time Management Strategies

Effective time management is crucial for building skills, especially when you have extra learning commitments in addition to your usual responsibilities.

Here are some strategies to help:

- **The Pomodoro Technique:** Work in focused blocks of 25 minutes followed by a 5-minute break. This method helps maintain concentration and prevent burnout. It's particularly effective for study sessions or when learning new skills.
- **Task Prioritisation:** Use tools like the Eisenhower Box to prioritise tasks based on urgency and importance. Allocate specific times for learning and treat these as immovable appointments.
- **Daily Routines:** Incorporate skill development into everyday activities. Listen to educational podcasts during your commute or read industry-related articles during lunch breaks.
- **Delegation and Outsourcing:** Delegate tasks that don't require your specific skill set. This frees up more time for focused skill development.

Psychological Barriers

When it comes to skill stacking, psychological barriers can be just as challenging as practical ones. Doubts, fears, and feelings of inadequacy can easily undermine your motivation and progress. The good news is that these barriers can be overcome with the right mindset and support.

- **Imposter Syndrome:** As we learned in Chapter 10, this common barrier involves doubting your accomplishments and fearing being exposed as a fraud. Overcome this by understanding that learning is a process and expertise takes time to build.

- **Mentorship:** Engage with mentors who can provide guidance, knowledge, and emotional support. Mentors offer reassurance and practical advice from their experiences.

- **Supportive Learning Communities:** Join groups or communities focused on learning. These provide a motivating sense of solidarity and shared purpose.

- **Celebrating Small Wins:** Focus on incremental achievements rather than only outcomes. Set small, manageable goals and celebrate when you meet them. This builds confidence and maintains motivation.

- **Cognitive Restructuring:** Challenge and change destructive thoughts. Replace negative thoughts with more constructive or realistic ones. For example, instead of thinking, *"I'll never get this right,"* believe, *"Every attempt is a step toward learning and improvement."*

YOUR ROUTE TO SUCCESS

Skill stacking is more than adding a few new abilities to your toolbox—it's a deliberate strategy for personal and professional growth. By diversifying your skill set, you can increase your adaptability, boost your creativity, and enhance your problem-solving capabilities, making you more valuable in any role. The key is approaching this process with intention and a clear roadmap. From assessing your current abilities to engaging in continuous learning and seeking new challenges, skill stacking can unlock opportunities and accelerate your success.

Skill Assessment and Gap Analysis

The first step is to understand your current skill set and identify areas for improvement. Take a comprehensive inventory of your skills, analyse gaps, and set strategic goals for acquiring new competencies.

- **Initial Assessment:** List skills acquired through formal education, work experience, hobbies, and other activities.
- **Identifying Gaps and Synergies:** Identify areas where your skills could be enhanced or new skills could complement existing ones. For instance, a digital marketer might benefit from learning data analytics.
- **Setting Goals:** Set clear and achievable goals for acquiring new skills—Prioritise skills with the most significant potential to enhance your career or personal growth.

Engagement in Continuous Learning

Embrace a mindset of lifelong learning. Stay updated with industry trends and enhance your skills through formal education, online courses, mentorship, and varied professional experiences.

- **Formal Education:** Search online platforms like Thinkific, Udemy, or LinkedIn Learning for courses that match your skill development goals.
- **Mentorship:** Seek mentors who possess the skills you aspire to learn. Mentorship provides guidance, motivation, and an insider's perspective on developing and applying new skills effectively.
- **Varied Professional Experiences:** Look for opportunities within your current role to apply new skills or volunteer for projects that require skills outside your comfort zone.

Supporting a Learning Culture

Cross-training and rotational programs enhance your skills and foster a better understanding of the organisation.

- **Cross-training Initiatives:** Develop cross-functional secondment programs that allow you to work in different departments or roles.
- **Rotational Programs:** Implement rotational programs for new or high-potential employees, allowing them to work in various business areas.
- **Feedback Mechanisms:** Incorporate regular feedback sessions into your learning plan.
- **Iterative Learning Process:** Embrace an iterative approach to learning, where feedback continuously adjusts and refines learning objectives.

INSIGHTS FROM MY JOURNEY

As I've battled through the challenges of Imposter Syndrome, which I shared in Chapter 10, and embraced the Growth Mindset discussed in Chapter 11, one thing has consistently driven me forward: developing new skills. It's been a powerful way to accept and thrive in new challenges.

Whether I've been stepping into new roles, exploring entirely different industries, or working with a diverse range of clients, the ability to continually learn and stack new skills has given me a unique competitive edge. Each new skill I've developed has added value—not just to me personally but to the businesses I've worked with and the people I've coached. Skill stacking has been a crucial part of my growth strategy. It's allowed me to remain adaptable and creative in problem-solving, providing a fresh perspective and helping me stand out in an ever-changing business landscape. By continually learning and integrating new skills into my toolkit, I've found that I can offer something unique—a fresh approach to leadership, a new angle in coaching, or innovative solutions for my clients.

This approach has helped me stay competitive and made my work more rewarding and impactful. Developing a diverse skill set is one of the best ways to stay ahead and grow.

17. NAVIGATING DAILY ROUTINES

Skill stacking, as you've learned, is a potent tool for career development. However, its effectiveness relies heavily on the habits underpinning these skills. Habits, the small, repeated actions we perform every day, significantly influence our productivity, health, and overall wellbeing. By mastering the art of habit formation, you can ensure you consistently work towards your goals, using habits as a foundation for success and a catalyst for continuous improvement and innovation. This understanding should make you more aware and conscious of your daily routines and their impact on your life.

LEADING THE WAY

James Clear, a modern authority on the science of habit formation, has transformed how millions of people understand and implement habits. His approach, outlined in the bestselling book *Atomic Habits*, is refreshingly simple. It's based on the idea that minor, incremental improvements, when compounded over time, can lead to extraordinary results. This simplicity should reassure you that habit formation is not a complex process but a series of small, manageable steps that can lead to significant change.

Mastering the Art of Habit Building

James Clear's personal story is one of growth through habit-building. After a traumatic injury in high school derailed his plans to play baseball, Clear had to rebuild himself—both physically and mentally—using tiny, daily habits. Over time, these habits allowed him to regain strength, improve his academic performance, and become a successful entrepreneur, writer, and speaker.

Clear's philosophy, centred on the power of marginal gains, is universally applicable. When repeated daily, these tiny 1% improvements lead to significant transformations. Success, as Clear teaches, isn't about radical overnight changes but the accumulation of consistent, positive behaviours over time. This idea has resonated with millions, from top athletes and CEOs to people striving for personal development. It's a philosophy that includes you, making you part of a larger community striving for continuous improvement.

Habits as a Competitive Advantage

Clear's insights go beyond personal development. His work highlights how habits can serve as a competitive advantage in business. Whether improving productivity, fostering innovation, or creating a positive company culture, organisations can thrive by building solid and intentional habits. Clear has shown how leaders can inspire their teams to develop habits that drive long-term success, turning daily routines into powerful tools for growth.

Clear himself is a living example of this philosophy. Using habit-building techniques, he has grown his blog from a small platform to one with millions of readers. He turned *Atomic Habits* into a global bestseller, selling over 10 million copies. His journey demonstrates how consistently applying positive habits can compound extraordinary outcomes, not just in personal life but also in business and leadership.

The secret to success lies in your daily habits. If you want to improve, don't focus on radical transformations or grand gestures. Instead, start with small, manageable actions and commit to doing them consistently. As Clear says, *"You do not rise to the level of your goals; you fall to the level of your systems."* By mastering your habits, you can master your life.

NAVIGATING THE WHY

Understanding why habits form and how they influence our behaviour is crucial for leveraging them personally and professionally. Scientific and interdisciplinary studies on habit formation provide insights into the brain's workings, the mechanisms of habit loops, and their practical applications in business and leadership.

The Neuroscience

Habits are deeply rooted in your brain's wiring, specifically in the basal ganglia. This part of your brain is crucial for emotions, memories, and recognising patterns. When you repeat a behaviour enough times, it transitions from being a deliberate action managed by the prefrontal cortex (responsible for decision-making and complex thinking) to becoming an automatic habit controlled by the basal ganglia (responsible for making sure actions are smooth and automatic). This shift makes the behaviour quicker and easier to perform because it requires less mental effort. Consequently, your prefrontal cortex is freed to focus on new tasks and challenges.

The Habit Loop Mechanism

Have you ever wondered why some habits stick while others fade away? It all comes down to something called the Habit Loop

Mechanism. It's a simple yet powerful process our brains use to build habits that become second nature. Every habit follows the same primary loop: a cue triggers an automatic routine, which leads to a reward. The more your brain recognises that this loop provides something positive, the more automatic it becomes.

- **Cue:** A cue is a trigger that tells the brain to go into automatic mode and which habit to use. This could be anything from an environmental signal, like seeing your running shoes by the door (cue to go for a run), to a time of day, like a mid-afternoon slump (cue for a coffee break).
- **Routine:** Routine is the behaviour, which can be physical, mental, or emotional. It's the action you take automatically when you encounter the cue.
- **Reward:** The reward helps your brain decide if this particular loop is worth remembering for the future. Over time, if the loop successfully provides rewards, this path of cue, routine, and reward becomes increasingly automatic.

Neuroplasticity

Habit formation also involves changes in the brain's structure—a concept known as neuroplasticity. Each time a habit loop is completed, the connections between neurons in the habit loop strengthen. The more a habit is practised, the stronger and more automatic the behaviour becomes due to these reinforced neural connections.

Interdisciplinary Studies

Habit formation extends beyond neuroscience, drawing insights from psychology and behavioural economics to provide a more comprehensive understanding of human behaviour.

- **Psychology:** Psychological studies have emphasised the role of repetition and reinforcement in habit formation—for instance, B.F. Skinner's operant conditioning theory demonstrates how the consequences of a behaviour (rewards or punishments) influence the likelihood of that behaviour being repeated.
- **Behavioural Economics:** This examines how economic decisions are not always rational but can be highly influenced by habitual behaviour and cognitive biases. For example, the status quo bias—a preference for the current state of affairs—can often result from habitual thinking.

Practical Implications in Business

Understanding how habits form and function can powerfully impact business practices. Leaders who cultivate positive decision-making habits and foster continuous innovation set the foundation for organisational success.

- **Decision-Making Habits:** Leaders who develop strong decision-making habits, such as systematically evaluating pros and cons or regularly consulting diverse viewpoints, can enhance organisational agility. These habits ensure that decisions are swift and considerate of various perspectives, leading to more adaptive and responsive business strategies.
- **Habitual Innovation:** In businesses, fostering a culture where habitual behaviours include regular brainstorming sessions, continuous learning, and openness to experimentation can lead to sustained innovation. Such habits encourage ongoing improvement and adaptability to changing market conditions.

IT'S NOT ALL PLAIN SAILING

Building and maintaining new habits is a challenging process that often encounters obstacles. The journey to habit formation can be fraught with difficulties, from balancing multiple habits to overcoming psychological barriers. However, understanding these challenges and employing strategic solutions can help you navigate them effectively.

Prioritisation

Focusing on one habit at a time is crucial until it becomes relatively automatic. This approach reduces the cognitive load and increases the likelihood of success. For instance, establish a consistent exercise routine to start a fitness regime and then improve your diet by gradually incorporating dietary changes once this becomes a part of your daily life. Prioritising habits ensures that each new behaviour is given the attention it needs to become ingrained before moving on to the next.

Integration

Integrating multiple habits into a cohesive routine can help reduce the cognitive load associated with remembering to practice each one. For example, if you want to develop reading and exercise habits, you could listen to audiobooks or podcasts while working out. This method allows you to combine activities, making it easier to maintain multiple habits simultaneously. Creating a structured daily schedule that incorporates all desired habits seamlessly can also aid in this integration, making the overall process less overwhelming.

Psychological Barriers

Mental blocks and old routines can present significant challenges when forming new habits. Overcoming these barriers requires a combination of incremental learning and mindfulness practices to build resilience and adaptability.

- **Incremental Learning:** Break down the process into smaller, more manageable tasks to make the challenge less daunting and build confidence as each piece is mastered. For example, if you aim to develop a daily habit of writing, start by writing for just five minutes daily and gradually increase the duration.
- **Mindfulness Practices:** Mindfulness can increase awareness of your actions and help control impulses that deviate from new habit patterns. Meditation, deep breathing exercises, and mindful reflection can enhance your ability to stay present and focused.

Resilience Building

Developing resilience is about accepting setbacks as a natural part of growth and learning from them. When things don't go according to plan, it's essential to reflect on what caused the setback and make adjustments. For example, imagine you've set a goal to read for 30 minutes each day but keep missing your target due to a busy schedule. Instead of giving up, analyse why it's not working—maybe you're trying to read at a time of day when you're too tired. Adjust your approach by choosing a different time, like during your lunch break or before bed.

This flexibility is critical to long-term success. If one strategy isn't working, don't hesitate to try a new one. Adapting your plan to fit your routine, lifestyle, or energy levels increases the likelihood of sticking with it. The combination of resilience and adaptability helps you stay on track, even when challenges arise.

Intrinsic and Extrinsic Rewards

Utilise both intrinsic and extrinsic rewards to maintain motivation. Intrinsic rewards, such as the satisfaction of personal growth or the joy of learning something new, can provide a deep sense of fulfilment. Extrinsic rewards, such as treating yourself to something special after reaching a milestone, can offer additional motivation. Balancing both types of rewards can help sustain your commitment to new habits.

YOUR ROUTE TO SUCCESS

Creating new habits is a structured process that goes beyond mere willpower. It involves setting up a systematic plan that makes the habit stick by incorporating incremental steps, environmental design, and the cue-routine-reward mechanism. Additionally, leveraging technology and tools can provide essential support in habit formation.

Incremental Steps

Start creating new habits with small, manageable changes that are not overwhelming. This gradual approach helps make the habit more sustainable. For example, if you aim to build a habit of reading industry news, start with one article a day rather than attempting an entire publication. This small step is more achievable and can gradually increase as the habit becomes more ingrained.

Environmental Design

Modify your environment to facilitate the desired habit. For instance, place a water bottle at your desk to remind you to stay hydrated throughout the day. Similarly, set up a dedicated workspace to help cultivate a habit of regular work planning. By removing obstacles and making the desired action more convenient, you significantly increase the likelihood of success.

Cue-Routine-Reward Revision

The cue-routine-reward cycle is fundamental to habit formation. Identify a clear cue for your new habit, establish a simple routine following that cue, and reward yourself for completing the routine. For example, if your cue is the morning alarm, your routine might be a 10-minute exercise session, and your reward could be a healthy breakfast. Over time, this reward will help solidify the habit loop, making the behaviour automatic.

Technology and Tools

Leveraging technology can significantly assist in habit formation by providing reminders, tracking progress, and offering motivational insights. Various apps and tools are designed to support habit development and can be integral to maintaining consistency.

- **Habit-Tracking Apps:** Use apps that track habit development to provide reminders and motivational statistics to keep you focused on your goals.

- **Reminders and Notifications:** Set up reminders and notifications on your phone or computer to remind you of your new habits. For example, schedule a daily meditation reminder to ensure you set aside time for this practice, making it more likely to become a regular part of your routine.

- **Feedback Loops:** Create mechanisms to receive feedback on your behaviour. This can be through self-assessment tools, journaling, or feedback from peers. Constructive feedback helps you understand your strengths and areas needing improvement.

Community and Accountability

A supportive community can play a crucial role in sustaining habits. Engage with others who share similar goals to gain motivation, encouragement, and a sense of accountability. Pair up with a colleague or friend who has similar goals. This mutual support can keep motivation high and help you stay committed to your habit.

Participation in Groups

Groups that share your new habits to gain motivation and increase commitment through social reinforcement. For example, participate in a book club to enhance your reading habits or join a fitness group to motivate you to exercise regularly.

INSIGHTS FROM MY JOURNEY

Throughout my career, I've realised how essential building habits are to personal development. At different stages, I've had to develop and adjust my habits to ensure I'm making the most of what I have and where I am. Whether I was stepping into a new role or facing new challenges, my habits needed to evolve to keep me on track.

As I continue to grow my business, the habits I've been focusing on most are related to productivity and time management. These habits have allowed me to maximise the time I spend adding value to my clients, which has become one of my top priorities. By streamlining my day-to-day tasks and minimising distractions, I can dedicate more energy to the things that truly matter—coaching, strategic thinking, or solving problems.

18. STRENGTH IN CONNECTIONS

Imagine having a solid network that offers opportunities you might never find through conventional means. Building trusted relationships over time can lead to lucrative partnerships, valuable client leads, and insider knowledge about industry trends. A recommendation from a well-respected connection often carries more weight than any advertisement or anonymous review. These deep, trusted connections can transform the trajectory of your business.

Each person in your network brings unique experiences and knowledge, enriching your understanding of the world. By actively engaging with a diverse network, you expose yourself to various perspectives that can challenge your viewpoints and spark innovative thinking. Try organising regular brainstorming sessions with different groups in your network to tap into this collective wisdom. These interactions can inspire new ideas, refine your strategies, and solve complex problems you might not have considered otherwise.

LEADING THE WAY

Sara Blakely is a shining example of how effective networking and building solid connections can turn a simple idea into a billion-dollar empire. As the founder of Spanx, Blakely's journey to success wasn't just about innovation but about forging the right relationships that helped propel her business forward.

The Power of Persistence and Networking

Blakely's story began with a single idea: to create a better undergarment for women. With no background in fashion or business, she knew that getting her product into the right hands would be critical to her success. She began cold-calling buyers from major department stores, facing numerous rejections. However, Blakely's ability to network, build rapport, and maintain persistence paid off when she finally secured her first big order with Neiman Marcus. This initial success opened the doors to even more significant opportunities.

One of Blakely's most significant networking wins came when she sent a gift basket of Spanx products to Oprah Winfrey, hoping to catch her attention. Blakely knew that Oprah's endorsement could be transformative, and her intuition was correct. In 2000, Oprah named Spanx her *"Favourite Product of the Year,"* skyrocketing the brand's visibility and sales overnight. This critical connection demonstrated the importance of strategic networking and how one influential relationship can alter the trajectory of a business.

Building Relationships to Sustain Growth

Blakely's success didn't stop with her product. She continued cultivating relationships with critical fashion, media, and retail figures, ensuring Spanx's long-term growth and brand presence. Her focus on authentic, personal connections with her team, partners, and customers has been central to Spanx's enduring success. Blakely's belief in the value of relationships extends beyond business, as she has also become a mentor and supporter of other female entrepreneurs, fostering a community of innovation and collaboration.

Sara Blakely's story illustrates how crucial building a solid network can be to entrepreneurial success. Her ability to create and nurture connections opened doors and cemented Spanx as a household name. She harnessed the power of networking to gain exposure, secure valuable partnerships, and make a loyal customer base, proving that solid connections can be the foundation of lasting business success.

NAVIGATING THE WHY

Networking is more than just accumulating contacts. It's a complex mix of psychological, sociological, and economic factors influencing behaviour and professional outcomes. Understanding these scientific principles can help you build more effective relationships and strategically leverage your network.

Psychological Foundations

From a psychological standpoint, we tend to gravitate toward people who share similarities with us—whether it's background, interests, or professional experience. Understanding this natural bias can give you a strategic edge when expanding your network, allowing you to connect more deliberately and inclusively.

Emotional intelligence is the true cornerstone of effective networking. Empathy and strong social skills enable you to tune into others' emotions, leading to more genuine, meaningful interactions. Self-regulation ensures you stay composed and approachable, even in challenging situations, making it easier to connect and engage. And don't forget the power of reciprocity—when you offer value or support, people feel naturally inclined to return the favour, strengthening your relationships and deepening your connections over time.

Sociological Aspects

Networking is deeply rooted in sociological principles, explaining how social structures and relationships influence our interactions. Social capital theory differentiates between bonding social capital, derived from close-knit relationships like those with family and close friends, and bridging social capital from looser, more diverse connections that provide new information and opportunities. Your network structure often dictates its usefulness; dense networks support and reinforce norms, while sparse networks offer diverse information and unique opportunities. Research shows that individuals with broader and more varied networks tend to have faster and more successful career trajectories, highlighting the importance of consciously building and nurturing a vast network.

Economic Implications

Economics plays an influential role in shaping the benefits and dynamics of networking. The concept of network effects suggests that the value of your network increases exponentially as it grows. A more extensive, diverse network gives you greater visibility, influence, and access to critical industry insights and trends. Effective networking also helps bridge information gaps—reducing information asymmetry by ensuring everyone has access to valuable knowledge, empowering you and your network to make more informed decisions.

Resource exchange theory adds another layer of value, highlighting how networks enable the flow of resources such as information, skills, and opportunities. Engaging in this exchange benefits all parties, fostering mutual growth and collaboration.

Understanding these economic dynamics allows you to leverage your network strategically, positioning yourself to negotiate, collaborate, and thrive.

IT'S NOT ALL PLAIN SAILING

While networking offers numerous benefits, it also presents challenges that can hinder your ability to connect effectively with others. Understanding and navigating these challenges is essential for building and maintaining a robust professional network.

Cultural Differences

Cultural differences can significantly impact your networking efforts in a global business environment. Ignoring or misunderstanding cultural nuances can lead to miscommunications and strained relationships. For example, business etiquette varies widely across cultures—what is considered polite and respectful in one country might be perceived differently in another. Invest time in learning about your contacts' cultural backgrounds. This includes understanding their communication styles, business practices, and social norms.

Digital Networking Challenges

Digital communication has transformed networking, introducing both opportunities and challenges. Navigating the nuances of digital communication, maintaining privacy, and managing an online persona are modern challenges that require careful consideration.

Digital etiquette is more than just polite language; it involves understanding the medium and the audience. Tailor your communication style to the platform—LinkedIn messages should be more formal, while Twitter might allow for a lighter tone. Respond promptly to messages and emails; timely responses show respect for others' time and foster positive relationships.

Maintaining Connections

Building a network is the first step; maintaining it requires ongoing effort and strategy. Regular and meaningful interactions are essential to keep your relationships strong and beneficial. Develop a plan for regularly contacting your connections. Use tools like CRM software or a simple spreadsheet to track interactions. Set reminders to reach out to contacts every few months to keep the relationship alive. When checking in, ensure your communication is meaningful. Share specific articles, videos, or events that align with their interests or needs. Personalised communication shows that you value the relationship beyond just professional gain.

Overcoming Networking Fatigue

Networking can sometimes feel overwhelming, especially when managing numerous contacts. Recognising and addressing networking fatigue is essential to maintain adequate and positive interactions. Focus on the most valuable connections that offer mutual benefit. This will help you manage your energy and resources more effectively. Establish realistic networking goals that align with your capacity and objectives. This prevents burnout and ensures sustained effort. Allow yourself to take breaks from networking when needed. Brief periods of rest can rejuvenate your enthusiasm and improve your interactions.

YOUR ROUTE TO SUCCESS

Mastering networking skills is crucial for enhancing your business success. Effective networking involves more than just exchanging business cards; it requires strategic relationship building, active engagement, and a keen understanding of social dynamics. Developing practical networking skills is an ongoing process that requires intentionality, strategy, and adaptability. By building quality relationships, leveraging both traditional and digital platforms, and continuously engaging with your network meaningfully, you can maximise the potential of your professional connections.

Strategic Relationship Building

Cultivate deeper relationships with a smaller group of contacts rather than spreading yourself too thin. More profound connections are more likely to yield substantial and meaningful exchanges that can lead to long-term benefits for all parties involved. Building a solid personal brand is essential in networking because it reflects who you are and what you stand for. Start by identifying your unique strengths and the values you want to communicate to your network. Consistently showcase these through your professional attire, communication style, and online presence.

Attending Industry Events

To expand your network, actively participate in industry conferences, seminars, and workshops. These are prime venues to meet like-minded people who share your interests and ambitions. Make a point of conversing with speakers and participants, exchanging contact information, and discussing potential collaboration opportunities.

Online Platforms

Leverage platforms like LinkedIn not just for connecting but for engaging with others. Share articles, comment on posts relevant to your field, and join groups that align with your business interests. This activity increases your visibility and helps establish your expertise in your field.

Volunteering and Boards

Consider volunteering for leadership roles in industry associations or local business groups. These positions often provide access to a network of influential people outside your immediate circle, enhancing personal growth and professional opportunities.

Reciprocity

Always look for opportunities to help others in your network. If someone introduces you to a valuable contact, think about who you could return the favour. You can also share opportunities, such as job postings or speaking engagements, which may benefit your contacts. Record interactions where you've received assistance and make a conscious effort to reciprocate. This might be as simple as recommending or sharing their business's social media posts. Acts of goodwill don't go unnoticed and often lead to more robust, loyal relationships.

Diversity and Inclusivity

Embrace diversity in your networking efforts by contacting professionals from various industries, cultural backgrounds, and career stages. Diverse networks can provide broader insights and expose you to new opportunities that a more uniform group might not. For instance, attending meetups or conferences focused on diversity in your industry can be a great way to expand your horizons. When engaging with people from different backgrounds, be open to learning about their experiences and perspectives. This enriches your understanding and strengthens your relationships through respect and mutual interest.

Soft Skills Development

Solid soft skills greatly enhance networking. Work on your active listening skills by focusing entirely on the other person during conversations without planning your response while they are speaking. This can lead to deeper understanding and more meaningful connections. Additionally, practice empathy by considering other people's perspectives and emotional states during interactions. This can be especially important in networking settings where building trust quickly is beneficial. Attending workshops or reading books on emotional intelligence can further enhance these skills.

INSIGHTS FROM MY JOURNEY

One of the things I've always enjoyed is connecting with new people. My natural curiosity has allowed me to approach networking with genuine interest, wanting to learn more about the individuals I meet. Over time, though, I've discovered that the real strength of networking doesn't just lie in making those initial connections—it's about connecting people who can help each other resolve challenges and solve problems.

One of the most rewarding aspects of networking is acting as a bridge, bringing together individuals whose skills, experiences, or insights complement one another. Finding the right person at the right time to create solutions is a powerful way to add value to those around you, and it's made infinitely more effective by having a robust and diverse network.

I've learned that networking isn't just about who you know—it's about how you connect with others and create opportunities for them to collaborate and grow. This thoughtful, intentional approach to building and nurturing networks has helped me and others achieve lasting success.

SECTION THREE

BEYOND THE HORIZON

19. YOUR FUTURE HISTORY

Imagine vividly seeing your business's future, with milestones, successes, and challenges ahead. This is the power of visualisation—a tool that can transform your business strategy and how you approach your future history.

Visualisation isn't just a personal tool; it's a powerful way to align your team's efforts. Like athletes who use visualisation to boost their performance, you can leverage it to turn abstract ideas into concrete plans. By visualising, you can foresee potential challenges and create a shared vision that guides your team. Regularly picturing your business goals, discussing them with your team, and mapping out the steps to achieve them can make them feel more natural and attainable. This practice helps keep everyone focused, motivated, and aligned, driving your business toward success.

LEADING THE WAY

As one of the most accomplished Formula 1 drivers in history, Lewis Hamilton has consistently demonstrated the power of mental preparation and imagery in a sport where split-second decisions can determine victory or defeat.

The Power of Mental Imagery

Throughout his illustrious career, Hamilton has relied heavily on visualisation techniques to prepare for races. Long before he hits the track, he spends time mentally rehearsing every corner, turn, and straight of the circuit. Hamilton visualises his lines, braking points, and overtaking strategies, allowing him to anticipate every possible scenario. This mental preparation helps him stay calm under pressure, knowing that he's already played out the race in his mind.

Hamilton has spoken about how visualisation helps him control his emotions and reactions during high-pressure moments. The intensity of Formula 1 requires more than physical skill—it demands psychological fortitude. By visualising his races, he creates a sense of familiarity with the track and competition, enabling him to remain composed, even when things don't go as planned. This psychological advantage has been a significant factor in his ability to make quick, decisive moves during crucial moments of a race.

Consistency at the Highest Level

In a sport where fractions of a second make all the difference, Hamilton's dedication to visualisation and mental preparation has been a critical component of his dominance. It's no coincidence that he's a seven-time Formula 1 World Champion. His consistency, adaptability, and ability to thrive under pressure have been enhanced by his commitment to mental training, which includes visualising everything from the perfect lap to how he'll manage unpredictable race-day conditions like weather or mechanical issues.

Hamilton's approach to preparation extends beyond just visualising the technical aspects of the race. He also mentally prepares for the crowd's energy, the intensity of competition, and even setbacks. This holistic approach to visualisation has allowed him to develop mental resilience, an essential skill in a physically and mentally taxing sport.

A Symbol of Mental Fortitude

Hamilton's story underscores the importance of mental strength in achieving greatness. His visualisation shows success is about physical ability, mental clarity, and preparedness to meet challenges head-on. His mindset has set him apart as a true leader in the sport, inspiring others to adopt similar practices in their personal and professional lives. By mentally preparing for every eventuality, you can build the confidence to execute under pressure and the resilience to bounce back when things go wrong.

NAVIGATING THE WHY

Visualisation is deeply rooted in cognitive science and psychology. When visualising a goal or scenario, your brain processes these mental images similarly to authentic experiences. This mental rehearsal can create neural patterns that enhance your ability to perform in similar real-life situations. Visualisation can transform abstract ideas into concrete strategies, making it a powerful tool for business leaders aiming to drive their organisations towards success.

Cognitive and Neurological Foundations

When visualising an action or outcome, your brain activates the same neural pathways as during actual performance. This process, known as neural mirroring, strengthens the connections within your brain, making the desired actions more familiar and more accessible to execute. Neuroscientific studies show that athletes who regularly practice visualisation can improve their performance almost as much as those who engage in physical practice. The brain doesn't differentiate much between a vividly imagined experience and a real one, reinforcing the neural circuits involved in the activity.

Psychological research underscores the benefits of mental rehearsal through visualisation. Repeatedly visualising success can enhance motivation, boost confidence, and reduce anxiety. This form of mental practice creates a positive mindset, preparing you to handle challenges more effectively and stay focused on your goals. For example, students who visualise their success in exams perform better, as the mental rehearsal helps them manage stress and approach the task positively.

The psychological impact of visualisation extends beyond performance enhancement. It also contributes to mental wellbeing by reducing stress and anxiety associated with high-stakes business decisions. Visualisation provides a mental rehearsal that prepares you for various scenarios, making you feel more in control and less apprehensive about potential challenges. This mental preparedness is crucial for maintaining composure and resilience in adversity.

Impact on Business Performance

Visualisation can significantly enhance business performance by making complex strategies more transparent and manageable. When leaders use visualisation, they can break down their plans into smaller, achievable steps, making it easier to communicate these plans to their teams. For example, if you envision the launch of a new product, you can picture each stage from development to market release. This mental roadmap helps spot potential problems early and develop solutions ahead of time, leading to a smoother implementation.

By mentally exploring various scenarios and outcomes, you can anticipate challenges and develop strategies to tackle them. This forward-thinking approach boosts decision-making and reduces the risk of unexpected issues disrupting the project. For instance, if you visualise a new competitor entering the market, you can mentally test different strategies to stay ahead, preparing your business to react quickly and effectively.

Visualisation also plays a crucial role in improving team coordination. When you and your team visualise your roles and how you contribute to a shared goal, it fosters unity and clarity. This shared vision helps align efforts, reduces misunderstandings, and enhances teamwork. For example, visualising a project's successful outcome helps team members understand their specific roles, leading to better coordination and execution.

Lastly, visualisation is a powerful tool for boosting confidence. By mentally seeing yourself succeed, you can create a sense of familiarity and assurance that prepares you for real-life challenges. For instance, an entrepreneur who visualises a successful pitch to investors can approach the presentation more confidently, having already mentally rehearsed and fine-tuned their approach.

IT'S NOT ALL PLAIN SAILING

While visualisation can be a powerful tool for achieving success, mastering it is challenging. From maintaining consistency to overcoming scepticism, developing a solid visualisation practice requires dedication and adaptability.

Maintaining Consistency

One of the biggest challenges in visualisation is maintaining a consistent practice. The initial enthusiasm can wane, and visualisation's effectiveness decreases without regular reinforcement. Consistency is crucial for embedding visualisation into your daily routine and ensuring it has a lasting impact.

- **Routine Integration:** Incorporate visualisation into your daily schedule. Set aside specific times each day for visualisation exercises, making them a non-negotiable part of your routine.
- **Accountability Partners:** Pair up with a colleague or mentor who can hold you accountable. Regular check-ins can help ensure you stay committed to your visualisation practice.

Overcoming Scepticism

Visualisation can sometimes be met with scepticism within yourself and others. Doubts about its effectiveness can hinder your ability to embrace and benefit from the practice entirely.

- **Educate and Inform:** Learn about the science and success stories behind visualisation. Understanding the evidence and hearing about real-world applications can help reinforce your belief in its power.
- **Track Progress:** Keep a journal to document your visualisation exercises and the outcomes. Seeing tangible results over time can help dispel doubts and strengthen your commitment.

Avoiding Burnout

Intense focus on visualisation without proper balance can lead to burnout. Maintaining a healthy approach is essential to ensure long-term sustainability.

- **Balanced Approach:** Balance visualisation with other activities that promote wellbeing, such as physical exercise, hobbies, and relaxation. This holistic approach helps maintain enthusiasm and energy.

- **Scheduled Breaks:** Recharge by taking regular breaks from intense visualisation sessions. Short pauses can refresh your mind and improve the overall quality of your practice.

Sustaining a Robust Visualisation Practice

To sustain a robust visualisation practice over the long term, it's essential to embed it into your business and continuously evolve your approach. The initial excitement of visualisation can often wane, making it crucial to have strategies in place that ensure consistency and growth.

- **Business Integration:** Foster an environment where visualisation is valued and practised collectively. Encourage team members to engage in visualisation exercises and share their visions regularly.
- **Continuous Learning:** Stay informed about the development of new visualisation techniques and tools. Attend workshops, read relevant literature, and experiment with new approaches to keep your practice fresh and compelling.
- **Support Systems:** Leverage support systems such as mentors, coaches, and peer groups. These networks can provide valuable feedback, encouragement, and accountability.

YOUR ROUTE TO SUCCESS

Developing and maintaining strong visualisation skills is a game-changer for transforming your business vision into reality. By integrating these insights, you can enhance your visualisation practice and feel confident and prepared for your strategic planning.

Holistic Visualisation

Successful visualisation goes beyond just picturing end goals. It involves a comprehensive view that includes the journey, potential obstacles, and the impact on all stakeholders. This holistic approach ensures that all aspects of a plan are considered, leading to more effective execution.

- **Comprehensive Planning:** Visualise the end goal and the steps needed. Consider potential challenges and how to overcome them. This approach reassures you that you have considered all aspects of your goal and instils confidence in your ability to execute your strategy effectively.
- **Stakeholder Impact:** Consider how your vision affects all stakeholders, including employees, customers, and partners. This broader perspective helps create more inclusive and sustainable strategies.

Driving Innovation and Creativity

Visualisation consistently drives innovation and creativity by allowing you to see possibilities beyond reality. This mindset is crucial for businesses looking to disrupt markets and create new opportunities.

- **Bold Thinking:** Use visualisation to explore unconventional ideas and potential breakthroughs. This can inspire bold thinking and experimentation within your team.
- **Creative Exercises:** Regularly engage in visualisation exercises that challenge the status quo and encourage innovative solutions. This practice fosters a culture of continuous improvement and creativity.

Building Resilience

Visualisation also builds resilience by mentally preparing for challenges and setbacks. By anticipating difficulties, you can develop strategies to overcome them, maintaining focus and motivation even in tough times.

- **Mental Rehearsal:** Visualise potential obstacles and practice handling them. This preparation helps you stay composed and practical under pressure.
- **Strategic Adjustments:** Regularly update your visualisation based on new information and changing circumstances. This flexibility ensures that you remain resilient and adaptable.

Define Your Vision

Clarity is critical to effective visualisation. Start by clearly defining your vision and articulating what success looks like for your business in specific, measurable terms. This clarity eliminates ambiguity, providing a focused path that guides decision-making and strategic planning.

- **Specific Goals:** Outline primary goals and milestones that signify progress. The more detailed and exact your vision, the easier it is to visualise and achieve.
- **Engage All Senses:** When visualising, engage all your senses to make the experience vivid and real. This multisensory approach creates a stronger neural imprint, making the visualisation more impactful and memorable.

Create Visual Aids

Visual aids such as vision boards and flowcharts are potent tools for representing your goals visually. These tools help keep your vision at the forefront of your mind and facilitate better understanding and communication of complex plans.

- **Vision Boards:** Gather images, quotes, and symbols that resonate with your vision and arrange them on a board. Place this board where you can see it daily to reinforce your goals and stay motivated.
- **Flowcharts and Diagrams:** Use flowcharts to map strategic plans and identify steps, processes, and potential challenges. This visual representation ensures that every aspect of your plan is considered and facilitates better communication with your team.

Use Technology

Leverage technology to enhance your visualisation practice. Simulation tools and data visualisation software can provide immersive experiences and transform raw data into actionable insights.

- **Simulation Tools:** Use virtual reality (VR) to create simulations of business scenarios. These immersive experiences help refine strategies before actual implementation.
- **Data Visualisation:** Utilise tools to transform complex datasets into understandable insights. This aids in strategic decision-making and planning.

INSIGHTS FROM MY JOURNEY

Later in life, I recognised visualisation as a critical driver of success, even though I'd been using it for years without fully realising it. Looking back, I can see how visualisation has played a role in many areas of my career, but one example that stands out is my speaking engagements.

Before I step in front of an audience, I often visualise the entire experience. I picture myself standing on stage, delivering my content and emphasising the key messages I want to convey. I imagine the audience's reactions—the engagement, the feedback, and hopefully, the positive impact my words will have. This visualisation process helps me feel more prepared, confident, and focused, allowing me to deliver with clarity and purpose.

I've found that mentally rehearsing these scenarios helps me anticipate potential challenges and prepare myself to adapt. Visualisation has become a crucial part of my approach, not only in public speaking but also in shaping the future of my business. It's a tool that helps me bring abstract ideas to life and turn them into concrete actions that drive success.

20. SCANNING THE HORIZON

How often do you look beyond the immediate horizon to anticipate changes that could impact your business? Many leaders focus on short-term goals and immediate challenges, leaving them vulnerable to unexpected market shifts. Horizon scanning bridges this gap by providing a comprehensive view of potential future scenarios, enabling you to make informed decisions and stay ahead of the curve.

Anticipating and adapting to future challenges and opportunities is crucial for long-term success. Horizon scanning is a strategic technique that allows you to systematically explore and analyse potential trends, disruptions, and emerging issues. By examining signals of change in the external environment, you can uncover trends that may influence your operations, market position, and competitive landscape. This foresight lets you develop flexible strategies that can be adapted as new information becomes available, ensuring your business remains resilient and forward-thinking.

LEADING THE WAY

Tim Urban, the creative mind behind the wildly popular blog *Wait, But Why*, is a modern-day example of someone who excels at horizon scanning. Urban has built his platform by exploring and explaining complex, future-oriented topics, ranging from artificial intelligence and space colonisation to the societal impact of emerging technologies. With a unique ability to break down abstract concepts, Urban helps his audience understand the long-term implications of developments that may seem far-off or hypothetical.

Anticipating the Future

Urban's horizon scanning goes beyond predicting technological advancements; it's about delving into the potential long-term consequences of those advancements for society and humanity. In his deep-dive blog posts, he has tackled Elon Musk's ventures into space exploration, AI, and renewable energy, showing how these innovations could shape the world over the next few decades. By focusing on the broad view, Urban gives his readers a glimpse into potential futures that could reshape industries and everyday life.

Connecting the Dots

Tim Urban has also proven adept at identifying change signals and connecting them to broader social and economic trends. Whether it's the future of digital communication or the ethical dilemmas posed by AI, his ability to anticipate and communicate these shifts has made *Wait, But Why* a go-to source for thought-provoking insights. Urban continually asks critical questions about how these emerging trends might interact, converge, or diverge, helping businesses and individuals better prepare for the future.

Urban's work shows that effective horizon scanning is not just the domain of scientists or business strategists—it can be a skill for anyone willing to explore, learn, and critically engage with the world around them. His approach encourages leaders and entrepreneurs to look beyond immediate concerns, using foresight and strategic thinking to prepare for the long-term changes shaping their industries. Urban's systematic exploration of future trends is a powerful reminder that successful businesses and individuals can anticipate and adapt to what's coming next.

Dedicating time to exploring and understanding your industry's horizon can unlock potential opportunities. Whether leading a startup or managing a team, investing in horizon scanning can help you stay ahead of the curve and anticipate the changes that will define the future.

NAVIGATING THE WHY

Horizon scanning involves systematic methods for identifying, analysing, and interpreting change signals in the external environment. It draws from various scientific disciplines, including strategic foresight, environmental scanning, and systems thinking. These methods help you anticipate future developments, understand their potential impacts, and effectively devise strategies to address them.

Strategic Foresight

Strategic foresight combines strategic planning with future studies, helping you anticipate and prepare for potential futures. It involves identifying long-term trends, envisioning multiple scenarios, and developing strategic responses. Research shows that companies using strategic foresight are better equipped to navigate uncertainty and achieve sustainable growth. For example, a study by the University of Manchester found that organisations that engage in foresight activities are more likely to innovate and perform better financially.

One key component of strategic foresight is scenario planning, where you create detailed and plausible future scenarios based on current trends and uncertainties. This technique allows you to explore potential futures and develop flexible and robust strategies across various scenarios. Trend analysis is another vital aspect of studying patterns and trajectories in data to predict future developments. By analysing trends in technology, consumer behaviour, and regulatory changes, you can make informed decisions that position your business advantageously for future challenges and opportunities.

Environmental Scanning

Environmental scanning involves continuously monitoring the external environment for trends and signals that could impact your business. This approach uses tools to categorise and evaluate external forces. Regularly conducting environmental scans lets you stay informed about changes in your external environment and adjust your strategies accordingly.

PESTEL analysis helps you categorise and evaluate the external forces that could impact your operations. This framework covers six critical areas—Political, Economic, Social, Technological, Environmental, and Legal—each of which can profoundly shape your business environment. For instance, changes in political regulations, such as new trade policies or tax reforms, can directly affect your operating costs or market accessibility. Economic conditions, like inflation, interest rates, or currency fluctuations, may impact consumer spending patterns or your financial health. Meanwhile, technological advancements can either provide a competitive edge through innovation or render existing products and processes obsolete if you're slow to adapt.

Social factors—such as evolving customer expectations, demographic shifts, or societal values—also play a crucial role in shaping demand and influencing brand perception. Environmental concerns, including climate change and sustainability practices, are becoming increasingly important, particularly as regulatory bodies impose stricter guidelines and consumers demand more eco-conscious products. Lastly, legal changes, such as updates to employment law, intellectual property rights, or industry-specific regulations, can pose risks or create new avenues for growth, depending on how quickly your business responds.

Regularly conducting PESTEL analyses ensures that you remain aware of these dynamic external forces, enabling you to respond proactively rather than reactively. You can better understand your business's strategic position by combining this external environmental scanning with internal assessments, such as SWOT (Strengths, Weaknesses, Opportunities, Threats) analysis. This integrated approach allows you to align your internal capabilities with external opportunities and threats, ensuring your business remains resilient, agile, and well-positioned to capitalise on emerging trends while mitigating risks.

Systems Thinking

Systems thinking provides a holistic view of how various factors interact within a more extensive system. It emphasises understanding the interconnectedness of different elements and how changes in one area can ripple through the entire system. Systems thinking helps you recognise your environment's complex and dynamic nature, allowing for more informed and effective decision-making.

Causal loop diagrams are tools used in systems thinking to visualise the relationships between different elements within a system. These diagrams help identify feedback loops and potential leverage points for intervention, enabling you to anticipate and mitigate unintended consequences. Dynamic modelling involves creating simulations of complex systems to explore how changes in one part of the system can affect the whole. This approach allows you to test different strategies and understand their potential impacts before implementing them in the real world.

Impact on Business Performance

Horizon scanning enables you to be ahead of the curve rather than reacting to changes, significantly improving your agility and resilience. Businesses that systematically scan their environments, shaping their future rather than being shaped by it, are better positioned to innovate, adapt, and thrive in a dynamic market.

Implementing early warning systems, the backbone of horizon scanning, is a strategic move that can alert you to emerging risks and opportunities. These systems, which monitor key indicators and trends, are instrumental in helping you take timely action to mitigate threats and capitalise on opportunities, thereby enhancing your strategic agility. Organisations that engage in horizon scanning, powered by these early warning systems, are more agile and resilient. You can adapt quickly to disruptions and maintain a competitive edge by anticipating changes and preparing for multiple scenarios. This proactive approach, fostered by the practical application of early warning systems, drives a culture of continuous improvement and innovation, paving the way for long-term success.

IT'S NOT ALL PLAIN SAILING

Implementing horizon scanning comes with its own set of challenges, but recognising these obstacles and knowing how to navigate them is vital to making the process successful. By identifying the most common hurdles upfront, you can develop proactive strategies to overcome them and ensure your business stays ahead of the curve.

Information Overload

The sheer volume of information available can be overwhelming. To manage this, quality should be prioritised over quantity, and the most relevant sources should be focused on. Use filtering techniques and tools to streamline the scanning process.

- **Prioritisation:** Identify your business's most critical areas and prioritise information sources that provide valuable insights into these areas. This focused approach ensures that you are not overwhelmed by irrelevant data.
- **Filtering Techniques:** Implement filtering techniques such as keyword searches, alerts, and content curation to sift through large volumes of information. Using tools like Google Alerts, RSS feeds, and specialised industry communications can help you stay updated on pertinent trends without becoming inundated.
- **Data Management Tools:** Utilise data management and analytics tools to organise and analyse information efficiently. These tools can help you visualise trends, identify patterns, and generate actionable insights from vast data.
- **Team Collaboration:** Encourage collaboration among team members to share the workload and insights. Designate specific individuals to monitor different areas, ensuring comprehensive coverage without overburdening anyone.

Bias and Subjectivity

Personal biases and subjective interpretations can skew the scanning results. To mitigate this, diverse perspectives must be involved, and structured methodologies must be used to ensure objectivity.

- **Diverse Perspectives:** Involve diverse individuals in the horizon-scanning process because different backgrounds, experiences, and viewpoints can provide a more balanced and objective analysis of trends and signals.
- **Structured Approach:** Employ structured approaches such as the Delphi method, where a panel of experts provides anonymous feedback and insights through multiple rounds of questioning. This process helps minimise individual biases and converges on a more objective consensus.
- **Cross-Verification:** Cross-verifying information from multiple sources is crucial in your horizon scanning process. It ensures the accuracy of your data and reduces the influence of bias. By triangulating data from different perspectives, you can gain a more comprehensive understanding of emerging trends.
- **Training and Awareness:** Equip your team with the necessary skills to recognise and mitigate cognitive biases. By raising awareness of common biases, such as confirmation or availability heuristics, you can empower individuals to critically evaluate information and make more objective assessments, enhancing the quality of your horizon scanning activities.

Resource Constraints

Horizon scanning can be resource-intensive, requiring time and expertise. To address this, allocate dedicated resources and consider outsourcing certain aspects to specialised firms or consultants.

- **Resource Allocation:** Allocate dedicated resources, including personnel and budget, to horizon scanning activities. Establish a team or designate individuals responsible for monitoring and analysing trends, ensuring they have the necessary tools and training.

- **Efficiency Strategies:** Optimise resource use by integrating horizon scanning into existing processes and leveraging technology. Automated tools and software can streamline data collection and analysis, reducing the manual effort required.
- **Outsourcing:** Consider outsourcing certain aspects of horizon scanning to specialised firms or consultants. These experts can provide advanced analytical capabilities, access to proprietary data, and additional perspectives that complement your internal efforts.
- **Scalable Processes:** Develop scalable processes that can grow with your business. Start with a focused approach and gradually expand as resources become available. Prioritise high-impact areas and continuously refine your methodologies.

YOUR ROUTE TO SUCCESS

Developing practical horizon-scanning skills is a theoretical exercise and a practical necessity. It involves intentional practice and adopting systematic approaches. By honing these skills, you can enhance your ability to anticipate and prepare for future challenges and opportunities, thereby gaining a competitive edge in the modern business landscape.

To maximise the effectiveness of your horizon scanning efforts, it is crucial to determine the key areas most relevant to your business. These areas might include technological advancements, regulatory changes, market trends, environmental factors, and societal shifts. Identifying these key areas will guide your horizon-scanning efforts and help you anticipate and prepare for future challenges and opportunities in your specific business context.

Strategic Focus

Begin by identifying your organisation's strategic priorities. Understanding these priorities will help you focus your scanning efforts on the most relevant areas. For instance, a technology company might prioritise scanning for emerging technologies and regulatory changes, while a consumer goods company might focus on market trends and consumer behaviour.

Tailor your horizon-scanning efforts to your business's specific needs. Different industries face unique challenges and opportunities, so it's essential to customise your approach accordingly. For example, the healthcare industry may need to focus on medical innovations and changes in healthcare policies, whereas the financial sector might prioritise economic indicators and regulatory developments.

Use Multiple Sources

Leverage various sources to gather information, including academic journals, industry reports, news outlets, social media, and expert opinions. Diverse sources provide a broader perspective and help identify weak signals of change.

- **Journals and Industry Reports:** These sources provide in-depth analysis and data on emerging trends and developments. Regularly reviewing these publications can offer valuable insights into the latest research and industry practices.
- **Traditional and Social Media:** Monitor news outlets and platforms to stay informed about current events and real-

time developments. These sources can provide immediate updates on changes that may impact your business.

- **Expert Opinions and Thought Leaders:** Engage with experts and thought leaders in your industry. Their insights and forecasts can help you understand potential future scenarios and the implications for your business. Attend webinars, listen to podcasts, and read blogs to stay connected with industry experts.

Engage with Networks

Participate in professional networks, conferences, and forums to stay informed about emerging trends and gain insights from industry peers. Engaging with thought leaders and experts can provide valuable foresight into future developments.

- **Professional Associations:** Join professional associations and industry groups to connect with peers and stay updated on the latest trends and developments. These organisations often host events, publish research, and facilitate networking opportunities.
- **Conferences and Workshops:** Attend meetings, workshops, and seminars to learn from experts and network with other professionals. These events provide a platform to exchange ideas, discuss challenges, and explore potential solutions.
- **Online Communities and Forums:** Participate in online communities and forums related to your industry. Discussions with peers and experts can provide new perspectives and insights into emerging trends and issues.

Regular Review and Reflection

Schedule regular reviews of your horizon-scanning efforts to assess their effectiveness and make necessary adjustments. Reflect on the insights gained and their implications for your business strategy.

- **Routine Reviews:** Establish a routine for reviewing your horizon-scanning activities. Quarterly or bi-annual reviews help ensure your scanning efforts align with your strategic objectives and capture relevant information.
- **Feedback Loops:** Implement feedback loops to gather input from team members and stakeholders. Their perspectives can help refine your scanning processes and identify any gaps or areas for improvement.
- **Continuous Improvement:** Horizon scanning is an ongoing process that requires constant refinement. Regularly reflect on the insights gained and their implications for your business strategy. Adapt your scanning efforts based on new information and evolving business needs.

INSIGHTS FROM MY JOURNEY

In my experience, Horizon Scanning has played a significant role in both the Hospitality industry and the third sector, albeit in very different ways. During my time in Hospitality, we always looked for the latest food and drink trends, ensuring we matched them to the right brand at the perfect time. These trends often start in London and slowly travel across the UK, with competitive socialising leading the way. Spotting these trends early and understanding when and how to introduce them gave us a competitive edge, allowing us to stay ahead of the curve.

But Horizon Scanning isn't just about finding the next big trend. In the third sector, where I'm involved with a charity, I've seen it take a more risk-focused approach. Here, it's used to protect essential services and secure funding for the future. Anticipating and proactively addressing potential risks ensures that the charity can continue to operate and serve its community, even in uncertain times.

This dual approach to Horizon Scanning—looking for opportunities while managing risks—has shown me the importance of foresight in any sector. Whether driving innovation or safeguarding against challenges, anticipating the future helps businesses and organisations thrive.

21. WORST CASE SCENARIO

Have you ever thought about how much smoother things could go if you could anticipate problems before they arise? This is where the pre-mortem technique comes in. Unlike traditional post-mortems, which analyse failures after they've happened, a pre-mortem involves imagining and analysing potential future failures before they occur. Doing this allows you to spot weaknesses, mitigate risks, and fine-tune your strategies to ensure success. The pre-mortem technique helps you shift from reactive to proactive, allowing you to foresee possible pitfalls and develop contingency plans. This foresight can help you distinguish between a minor setback and a major failure. By thinking ahead, you can build your resilience and flexibility, making your business better prepared for unexpected challenges.

LEADING THE WAY

Pixar Animation Studios, renowned for its groundbreaking films like *Toy Story, Finding Nemo, and Inside Out*, is celebrated for its creativity and rigorous and innovative approach to problem-solving. One of the critical elements of Pixar's success is its early adoption of a pre-mortem process to identify and mitigate potential issues before they become impossible. This foresight has enabled the studio to consistently deliver high-quality, commercially successful films that resonate with audiences worldwide.

Preventing Problems Before They Happen

At the core of Pixar's creative process is the *Braintrust*, a regular meeting of the studio's top directors, writers, and producers. In these meetings, the team critically reviews every project at various stages of development, openly discussing potential pitfalls, weak points in the story, and any technical or production challenges. This open and honest critique resembles a pre-mortem, where team members imagine the worst-case scenario for the film and work together to find solutions before issues derail production.

Unlike traditional feedback sessions, Pixar's *Braintrust* is built on candid communication and psychological safety, allowing team members to provide constructive criticism without fear of personal attack. This ensures that problems are identified early and possible failures are anticipated long before they affect the film's final product. The *Braintrust* sessions also focus on generating actionable solutions and turning potential failures into opportunities for improvement.

From Problem to Masterpiece

One of the best examples of Pixar's pre-mortem process in action is the production of *Toy Story 2*. Initially, the film faced significant issues, with story problems and technical hurdles threatening to derail the entire project. However, thanks to *Braintrust's* rigorous reviews and the team's commitment to candid problem-solving, Pixar was able to rework the story, fix the animation challenges, and transform *Toy Story 2* into one of the most successful sequels in film history.

Pixar's ability to engage in pre-mortem evaluations and anticipate potential failures long before they arise has been critical to its continued success. By embracing an environment of transparency and collaboration, Pixar consistently mitigates risks, turning potential setbacks into the building blocks of their most outstanding achievements.

Pixar's *Braintrust* is a testament to the power of pre-mortems in creative and business processes. The studio's willingness to confront potential failures head-on and foster an open, collaborative environment for critique allows it to produce technically brilliant films that resonate deeply with audiences. For leaders in any industry, Pixar's approach provides a valuable blueprint. By identifying weaknesses early and involving diverse perspectives in problem-solving, you can transform risks into opportunities for innovation and success.

NAVIGATING THE WHY

The pre-mortem technique is grounded in cognitive psychology and strategic foresight. It leverages our natural tendency to imagine worst-case scenarios, helping us identify potential risks and develop contingency plans. This method can enhance your strategic planning and risk management processes, leading to better outcomes.

Cognitive and Psychological Foundations

Psychologist Gary Klein, who coined the pre-mortem technique, found that imagining a failed project can significantly improve decision-making. This method, known as prospective hindsight, involves envisioning a future failure and then working backwards to determine the causes of that failure. By doing this, teams can think critically about potential pitfalls and take proactive steps to prevent those outcomes. This approach shifts your mindset from natural optimism to a more realistic evaluation of possible risks.

Pre-mortems help counteract common cognitive biases such as overconfidence and confirmation bias. Overconfidence can lead teams to underestimate risks, while confirmation bias can cause them to focus on information that supports their beliefs. By systematically exploring how things could go wrong, pre-mortems encourage a more balanced and realistic assessment of potential risks. Involving diverse perspectives in this process ensures a comprehensive analysis, as different team members may identify different risks based on their unique experiences and viewpoints.

Impact on Business Performance

Implementing pre-mortems can significantly enhance risk management. By identifying and addressing potential failures early, you can develop strategies to mitigate these risks before they escalate. This proactive approach reduces the likelihood of costly setbacks and ensures your organisation is better prepared to handle unexpected challenges. Pre-mortems can also help prioritise risks, enabling teams to focus on the most critical threats to their projects or business operations.

Pre-mortems foster a proactive approach to planning, allowing you to adapt your strategies based on identified risks and opportunities. This enhances overall agility and resilience, enabling you to respond more effectively to changing market conditions and external threats. Regularly conducting pre-mortems can refine your strategies, making them more robust and adaptable. This continuous improvement loop ensures that your organisation remains dynamic and can navigate complex and uncertain environments.

IT'S NOT ALL PLAIN SAILING

Implementing pre-mortems can present particular challenges, but thoughtful strategies can overcome these. Recognising and addressing these challenges is crucial for integrating the pre-mortem technique effectively into your business processes.

General Acceptance

Implementing pre-mortem sessions often meets with resistance due to their focus on potential adverse outcomes. This resistance typically stems from a misunderstanding of the technique's purpose. To overcome this, emphasise the proactive nature of pre-mortems, framing them as tools for ensuring project success rather than predicting failure. Highlight how pre-mortems can prevent issues before they arise, ultimately saving time and resources.

Gaining buy-in from leadership is also crucial. When leaders openly support and participate in these sessions, it underscores their importance and helps foster a culture that values risk anticipation as a critical component of strategic planning.

Facilitator Training

Effective facilitation is critical to productive pre-mortem sessions. Facilitators should be trained to keep discussions focused and constructive, avoiding unproductive negativity. They should encourage participation from all team members to ensure diverse perspectives are considered. A structured approach, including prepared templates, clear agendas, and defined participant roles, helps maintain focus and thoroughly examines all relevant areas.

Maintaining Morale

While it's important to consider potential failures, maintaining team morale is crucial—balance pre-mortem sessions with positive affirmations and discussions about the project's strengths and opportunities. Acknowledge past successes and the team's capabilities before delving into potential risks. Encourage a solution-oriented mindset by developing actionable strategies to mitigate identified risks, shifting the focus from problems to solutions, and reinforcing the team's ability to overcome challenges.

Optimism Bias

One challenge in pre-mortem sessions is balancing optimism with realism. Teams may naturally lean towards optimism, underestimating potential risks. To counteract this, emphasise the importance of realistic assessments grounded in data and past experiences. Involving diverse perspectives ensures a balanced view, as different team members may identify various risks and solutions based on their unique experiences and expertise. This diversity helps counteract individual biases and provides a more comprehensive risk assessment.

Commitment to Action

Develop clear action plans based on the insights from pre-mortem sessions, assigning responsibilities and timelines for implementing risk mitigation strategies. Ensure these plans are integrated into the overall project plan and regularly monitored. Holding team members accountable for following through on the mitigation strategies developed during pre-mortem sessions is crucial. Regular check-ins and progress reports help ensure that the identified risks are effectively managed.

YOUR ROUTE TO SUCCESS

Developing practical pre-mortem skills involves understanding and incorporating the methodology into your planning. By embedding this approach into your organisational culture, you can systematically anticipate and address potential failures, enhancing your strategic planning and risk management capabilities.

Practical Implementation

A pre-mortem needs to be structured to be effective. Start by clearly defining the project or decision at hand. Gather your team and explain the purpose of the pre-mortem. Ask each team member to envision that the project has failed and list all possible reasons for this failure. Collect these reasons, categorise them, and discuss potential mitigation strategies.

To maximise the benefits of pre-mortems, integrate them into your regular planning and review processes. Conduct premortems at the start of new projects, during significant decision-making processes, and at regular intervals throughout the project lifecycle. This ensures that potential risks are continuously monitored and addressed.

Conducting a Pre-Mortem

Incorporating pre-mortems into your strategic planning processes enhances your organisation's agility. By identifying potential obstacles early, you can pivot more effectively and make informed decisions that keep your projects on track. This proactive approach enables you to seize opportunities and mitigate real-time risks, ensuring your business remains competitive and resilient.

Here is a 7-step process to help you:

- **Define the Project:** Start by clearly defining the project or decision. Ensure that all team members understand the scope and objectives.

- **Cross-Functional Teams:** Involve team members from various departments and levels of the organisation to gather diverse insights. Different perspectives can help identify a broader range of potential risks.

- **Envision Failure:** Ask the team to imagine a disastrous project failure scenario. Encourage them to think critically about what went wrong.

- **Brainstorm Causes:** Facilitate a brainstorming session in which team members list all possible reasons for failure. Encourage open and honest discussion, emphasising that every idea is plausible.

- **Document Issues:** Compile a comprehensive list of potential issues. Categorise them based on severity and likelihood.

- **Develop Mitigation Strategies:** For each identified issue, brainstorm strategies to prevent or mitigate the potential failure. Assign responsibilities and timelines for implementing these strategies.

- **External Support:** Consider involving external consultants or industry experts to provide an outsider's perspective. Their impartial insights can uncover blind spots that internal teams might overlook.

Implementing Regular Pre-Mortems

To effectively integrate pre-mortems into your business processes, it's essential to take a structured and thoughtful approach. Seamlessly incorporating pre-mortem analysis into your regular workflow ensures it becomes a valuable tool for identifying and managing potential risks.

- **Routine Practice:** Incorporate pre-mortem analysis into your regular planning and review meetings to make it an integral part of your business strategy. This ensures that potential risks are consistently evaluated and addressed. For example, scheduling pre-mortem analyses at crucial project milestones or during quarterly strategic reviews helps maintain a proactive approach to risk management, keeping your team vigilant and prepared.
- **Project Templates:** Create standard project templates that include pre-mortem analyses as a required component. By embedding pre-mortems into your project planning, you ensure consistency across all projects, fostering a culture of foresight and preparedness throughout your organisation.
- **Skill Development:** Offer training and workshops on premortem techniques to enhance your team's ability to conduct practical sessions. Equip them with the necessary tools and methodologies, including principles of prospective hindsight, bias mitigation, and effective brainstorming techniques. Well-prepared team members are more likely to effectively identify and address potential risks, making the pre-mortem process more productive.

- **Simulated Exercises:** Conduct simulated pre-mortem exercises in a low-stakes environment to help team members become comfortable with the process. These simulations improve their ability to identify and address potential risks, making actual pre-mortem sessions more effective and productive. Practice sessions also help build confidence and refine techniques, ensuring better outcomes during actual pre-mortem analyses.

Creating a Supportive Environment

Creating a supportive environment is crucial for the success of pre-mortem sessions. Fostering a culture of openness and recognition encourages team members to actively participate and share valuable insights.

- **Encourage Openness:** To foster a culture where team members feel comfortable discussing potential failures, emphasise that pre-mortem sessions aim to improve project outcomes, not to criticise past mistakes. Creating a supportive environment that encourages candid discussions allows you to gather valuable insights that might remain unspoken.

- **Recognise Contributions:** Acknowledge and reward team members who actively participate in pre-mortem sessions and contribute valuable insights. Recognition motivates others to engage fully in the process, creating a more dynamic and collaborative environment where pre-mortem sessions thrive.

Continuous Improvement

Continuous improvement is essential for refining and ensuring the effectiveness of your pre-mortem processes. Gathering insights, iterating enhancements, and monitoring outcomes will help you enhance your pre-mortem practices.

- **Gathering Insights:** Implement structured feedback loops to collect insights from team members about the effectiveness of pre-mortem sessions. Use surveys, debrief meetings, and anonymous feedback tools to gather candid input on what worked well and areas needing improvement. This feedback provides a foundation for refining your approach.

- **Iterative Improvement:** Analyse feedback to identify patterns and areas for enhancement. For instance, if feedback indicates that sessions are too lengthy or lack focus, adjust the format to be more concise and structured. By continuously refining your approach based on feedback, you can improve the efficiency and effectiveness of future post-mortem sessions.

- **Monitor Outcomes:** Track the outcomes of projects that have undergone pre-mortem analyses to assess whether identified risks materialised and evaluate the effectiveness of mitigation strategies. Use these insights to continuously improve the process, ensuring that your pre-mortem sessions lead to better project outcomes and a more resilient organisation.

INSIGHTS FROM MY JOURNEY

The pre-mortem technique has become a cornerstone of my strategic planning approach, especially when developing new products, projects, or programmes. I've even applied this technique while planning this very book. The goal isn't to prevent things from going wrong entirely—that's unrealistic—but to use foresight to identify potential risks and mitigate them as much as possible.

In my experience, pre-mortems help me think critically about what could go wrong before starting. This mindset shift has allowed me to navigate uncertainties more confidently, making my business more resilient in facing challenges. It's about preparing for worst-case scenarios so that, if they do arise, I already have a plan to tackle them head-on.

22. DISRUPTING THE CALM

How often do you stick to the tried and tested because it's comfortable? While the status quo offers safety, it can stifle innovation and slow progress. To achieve lasting success, you need a mindset that challenges established norms. Like pirates who refused to accept traditional maritime laws, you must be willing to question and shake up industry standards. This could mean rethinking business models, innovating products or services, or embracing new technologies.

Breaking and rewriting the rules, redistributing power, harnessing a solid team, and taking decisive action can lead your business to new heights. Challenging the status quo isn't about being rebellious for the sake of it. It's about daring to innovate, pushing boundaries, and creating a culture of continuous improvement.

LEADING THE WAY

BrewDog, the Scottish craft beer company, is a perfect example of a business that has challenged the status quo and disrupted its industry in remarkable ways. Founded by James Watt and Martin Dickie in 2007, BrewDog was born out of frustration with what they saw as a bland and uninspiring beer market dominated by large corporations. They sought to create a bold and rebellious brand that would shake up the beer industry with innovative products, direct-to-consumer strategies, and a commitment to doing things differently.

Disrupting the Beer Industry

BrewDog's approach to brewing was unapologetically different. Instead of adhering to traditional beer styles, the founders focused on crafting bold, flavourful, high-quality beers that broke the mould. With beers like the iconic *Punk IPA*, BrewDog attracted a loyal following of beer enthusiasts looking for something more exciting than the mass-produced lagers that dominated supermarket shelves.

However, it wasn't just the beer that disrupted the industry; it was also BrewDog's attitude and marketing. From provocative branding to stunts like launching beers into space or brewing the world's strongest beer, BrewDog positioned itself as a rebellious, anti-establishment brand. This helped the company stand out in a crowded market and connect with younger consumers seeking authenticity and creativity in their beer choices.

Equity for Punks: Challenging Convention

One of BrewDog's most disruptive moves was its *Equity for Punks* initiative, which turned traditional business fundraising on its head. Instead of relying on conventional financing methods, BrewDog opened up investment opportunities to its customers and fans, allowing them to buy shares in the company through crowdfunding. This approach gave the company the capital to grow and helped build a dedicated community of shareholders who felt personally invested in the brand's success.

Equity for Punks has become a cornerstone of BrewDog's identity, with thousands of people owning shares and becoming brand ambassadors. By fostering this unique relationship between the company and its customers, BrewDog created a robust network of advocates who have helped spread the brand's message far and wide.

Sustainability and Social Responsibility

BrewDog's commitment to challenging the status quo goes beyond just brewing beer. The company has also positioned itself as a leader in sustainability within the industry. In 2020, BrewDog announced that it had become the world's first carbon-negative brewery, meaning it removes more carbon from the atmosphere than it emits. This bold move set a new standard for sustainability in brewing and showcased the company's willingness to take action on environmental issues.

BrewDog's rise from a small startup in Aberdeen to a global craft beer powerhouse is a testament to the power of challenging the status quo. Their journey demonstrates how businesses can succeed by embracing bold ideas, thinking outside the box, and staying connected to their customers.

NAVIGATING THE WHY

Psychology and organisational behaviour studies highlight the importance of questioning conventional practices to foster innovation, boost employee engagement, and maintain agility. Businesses can achieve disruptive innovation by challenging the status quo, often driving significant advancements.

Psychological and Organisational Benefits

Research reveals that challenging the status quo fosters innovation and drives business success. Companies encouraging disruptive thinking are more likely to develop groundbreaking products and services. Being open to new ideas is linked to higher levels of creativity, employee engagement, and organisational agility.

- **Creativity and Innovation:** When employees are encouraged to challenge the status quo, they are more likely to think creatively and propose innovative solutions. This environment nurtures a culture that values questioning and experimentation, leading to breakthrough ideas and advancements. Psychological research indicates that environments fostering psychological safety—where individuals feel safe to take risks and express their ideas without fear of negative consequences—significantly enhance creativity and innovation.

- **Employee Engagement:** Encouraging disruptive thinking positively impacts employee engagement. When employees feel their ideas are valued and are free to question and innovate, their job satisfaction and motivation increase. Engaged employees are likelier to go above and beyond, contributing to the organisation's success. Studies show that engaged employees are 87% less likely to leave their companies, highlighting the retention benefits of fostering an innovative culture.

Organisational Agility

Organisations challenging the status quo are more agile and better equipped to adapt to changing market conditions. These companies can swiftly pivot and respond to new opportunities and threats by constantly questioning and reassessing strategies and processes. This agility is crucial in today's fast-paced business environment, where the ability to adapt quickly can be a significant competitive advantage.

Innovation and Disruptive Thinking

Clayton Christensen introduced the idea of disruptive innovation, which is all about challenging established norms. This approach has the power to lead to significant advancements. Businesses that adopt a disruptive mindset are better equipped to anticipate market shifts and respond to emerging opportunities. This approach enhances competitiveness and positions companies as industry leaders.

- **Disruptive Innovation:** Disruptive innovation involves creating products or services that initially cater to a niche market but eventually disrupt established industries. This process often begins by challenging the assumptions and norms that dominate the industry. By thinking differently and exploring unconventional solutions, companies can identify gaps and opportunities that incumbents may overlook. Examples include personal computers, which revolutionised the computing industry, and ride-sharing services like Uber, which transformed taxi rides forever.

- **Market Shifts and Opportunities:** Businesses that embrace disruptive thinking are not just reactive to market shifts, they are proactive in identifying and capitalising on them. By constantly scanning for emerging trends and technologies, these companies can position themselves at the forefront of innovation. This proactive approach allows them to seize new opportunities before competitors, establishing themselves as market leaders. For instance, Amazon's continuous innovation in e-commerce, cloud computing, and logistics has enabled it to dominate multiple industries.

- **Competitiveness and Leadership:** Adopting a disruptive mindset is not just about the company, it's about the leaders who foster it. Companies can build a loyal customer base by continually challenging the status quo and seeking better ways to serve customers. Leaders who foster a culture of disruptive thinking inspire their teams to push boundaries and strive for excellence, instilling a sense of pride and accomplishment. This leadership approach drives business success and attracts top talent, as individuals are drawn to organisations that value innovation and creativity.

IT'S NOT ALL PLAIN SAILING

Challenging the status quo and fostering a culture of innovation come with challenges. Understanding and developing strategies to overcome these obstacles is crucial for successfully implementing disruptive changes.

Resistance to Change

Resistance to change is one of the most significant obstacles to challenging the status quo. Employees and stakeholders often feel comfortable with existing practices and may resist embracing new approaches. This resistance can stem from a fear of the unknown, a lack of understanding of the benefits of change, or simply a preference for the familiar.

- **Communicating the Benefits:** Communicate the benefits of change. Explain how new approaches can improve efficiency, innovation, and long-term success. Use data, case studies, and real-world examples to illustrate the positive impact of proposed changes.

- **Involving Team Members:** Involve team members in decision-making to foster a sense of ownership and buy-in. When employees feel their voices are heard and their contributions are valued, they are more likely to support and engage with new initiatives. Encourage open dialogue and solicit feedback to address concerns and build consensus.

- **Training and Support:** Provide training and support to help employees adapt to new approaches. Equip them with the skills and knowledge needed to implement changes effectively. Offer resources such as workshops, mentoring, and online courses to facilitate the transition.

Fear of Failure

The fear of failure is another significant barrier to disruptive thinking. Employees and leaders may hesitate to take risks or propose bold ideas due to potential failure and its perceived negative consequences. This fear can stifle creativity and prevent the organisation from pursuing innovative opportunities.

- **Cultivating a Growth Mindset:** Foster a culture that views failure as a learning opportunity rather than a setback. Encourage a growth mindset, where mistakes are seen as valuable experiences that contribute to personal and organisational growth. Emphasise the importance of resilience and adaptability in the face of challenges.

- **Encouraging Experimentation:** Create an environment that promotes experimentation and supports calculated risk-taking. Allow teams to test new ideas on a small scale before committing to more significant investments.

Celebrate the insights from unsuccessful attempts and use them to inform future strategies.

- **Recognising Efforts:** Recognise and reward innovation efforts regardless of the outcome. Highlight the importance of creativity and initiative and celebrate the innovation process as much as the results. This recognition can motivate employees to continue pushing boundaries and exploring new possibilities.

Balancing Innovation and Stability

While innovation is crucial for growth and competitiveness, maintaining stability in core operations is equally important. Striking a balance between these two priorities can be challenging but essential for sustainable success.

- **Gradual Implementation:** Implement changes gradually to ensure that core operations remain stable. Pilot new initiatives in specific areas or departments before rolling them out across the business. This approach allows for testing and refinement while minimising disruption to essential processes.

- **Strengthen The Foundations:** Ensure processes are solid and resilient before introducing significant changes. Conduct regular reviews and audits to identify areas for improvement and reinforce the stability of critical operations. A solid foundation provides a reliable platform for innovation.

- **Creating Clear Frameworks:** Establish clear frameworks and guidelines for balancing innovation and stability. Define criteria for prioritising initiatives, allocating resources, and assessing risk. These frameworks can help ensure that innovation efforts are aligned with the organisation's strategic goals and do not compromise core functions.

YOUR ROUTE TO SUCCESS

Cultivating a disruptive mindset is crucial for challenging the status quo and driving innovation within your business. This mindset encourages you to question existing norms, rethink established practices, and foster a culture that values creativity and boldness. Developing this approach involves several key strategies to transform how you and your team approach challenges and opportunities.

Break the Rules

To foster innovation, challenge conventional wisdom and question existing norms. Encourage yourself and your team to critically assess current practices and identify areas where traditional approaches may limit creativity and progress.

- **Questioning the Norms:** Hold regular brainstorming sessions, during which team members are encouraged to ask, *"Why are things done that way?"* and *"How can we do this better?"* This can uncover outdated practices that need to be revamped or replaced.
- **Encouraging Curiosity:** Promote a culture of curiosity where employees feel safe asking questions and proposing new ideas. Encourage them to explore and experiment with different methods and approaches.

Rewrite the Rules

Developing new, more effective ways of doing things can significantly improve efficiency, productivity, and innovation. This might involve rethinking your business model, redesigning processes, or introducing innovative products and services.

- **Innovative Business Models:** Consider alternative business models that better serve your market. For example, subscription-based services or platform-based models might offer more value than traditional sales approaches.
- **Process Redesign:** Analyse existing workflows to identify bottlenecks or inefficiencies. Implement process redesign initiatives to streamline operations, reduce waste, and improve overall performance.
- **Product and Service Innovation:** Invest in research and development to create or enhance existing products. Continuously innovate and adapt to customer needs to stay ahead of market trends.

Redistribute Power

Foster a culture of collaboration and shared leadership to enhance decision-making and drive innovation. Empowering team members to take ownership of their roles and contribute to decision-making can lead to more diverse perspectives and better outcomes.

- **Collaborative Leadership:** Encourage a leadership style that values input from all levels of the organisation. Create cross-functional teams to tackle complex challenges and leverage your organisation's diverse skills and knowledge.
- **Decentralised Decision-Making:** Empower employees to make decisions within their areas of expertise. This can speed up response times and enable more agile and adaptive operations.

Harness the Power of a Crew

Building strong, cohesive teams with a shared vision is crucial for fostering innovation and overcoming challenges. Encourage open communication, mutual support, and collective problem-solving.

- **Team Building:** Invest in team-building activities that strengthen relationships and trust among team members. Foster a sense of belonging and shared purpose to enhance collaboration and morale.

- **Open Communication:** Promote transparent and open communication channels within your organisation. Encourage team members to share their ideas, concerns, and feedback without fear of judgment.

- **Collective Problem-Solving:** Use collaborative tools and techniques, such as brainstorming sessions and design thinking workshops, to engage the team in solving complex problems together.

- **Experimentation:** Implement a culture of prototyping and experimentation. Allow teams to develop and test their ideas on a small scale before committing to more significant investments. This iterative approach reduces risk and fosters innovation.

INSIGHTS FROM MY JOURNEY

I've always embraced challenging the status quo, especially regarding how I approach consultancy. During my corporate career, I had a conventional view of what consultancy and advisory work should look like—typically focused on specific project engagements. However, I've always felt there was a better way to add value beyond just the project itself.

In my work now, I'm breaking away from that traditional model by focusing on developing long-term client partnerships. I believe that actual value isn't confined to the boundaries of a single engagement. This approach isn't typical in consultancy, but I've seen how it leads to more robust outcomes and greater client satisfaction. By fostering these partnerships, I'm able to help my clients navigate challenges and seize opportunities in ways that go beyond conventional consulting practices. This mindset of disrupting the calm—questioning what's always been done—drives innovation in my business and the businesses I work with.

23. MAPPING THE EXPEDITION

Strategic planning isn't just about setting a direction for your business; it's about creating a roadmap that guides you. It involves looking beyond the immediate horizon to anticipate future trends, potential obstacles, and emerging opportunities. By proactively addressing these factors, you can position your business to respond swiftly and effectively, ensuring sustained growth and resilience.

Moreover, strategic planning fosters alignment across all levels of your business. It ensures that every department and employee understands the company's goals and their role in achieving them. This alignment boosts morale, enhances productivity, and cultivates a culture of collaboration and innovation.

LEADING THE WAY

Emily Weiss, the visionary founder of Glossier, exemplifies how strategic planning can turn a niche idea into a billion-dollar business. Glossier revolutionised the beauty industry by prioritising customer engagement and a direct-to-consumer model, all driven by Weiss's strategic foresight and ability to anticipate trends before they became mainstream. Her approach to building Glossier highlights the power of thoughtful, long-term planning and execution.

Building a Brand Through Community

Weiss's journey started with her beauty blog, *Into the Gloss*, where she engaged directly with her readers, asking them about their skincare routines and beauty habits. This two-way communication allowed Weiss to identify a gap in the market—customers wanted skincare and makeup products that reflected their preferences rather than being dictated by traditional beauty brands. Using insights from her blog's loyal following, Weiss strategically planned Glossier around customer feedback, focusing on simple, practical products celebrating natural beauty.

This customer-first approach was a crucial part of Weiss's strategic vision. By understanding her audience's desires, she could build a product line that resonated deeply with her target market, allowing Glossier to stand out in a crowded beauty industry. Her decision to launch directly to consumers through e-commerce rather than traditional retail channels allowed Glossier to maintain a close relationship with its customers and scale quickly.

Long-Term Planning for Growth

Weiss's strategic planning didn't stop at product development. As Glossier grew, she focused on the long-term expansion of the brand, investing in digital marketing and building a community to keep customers engaged and loyal. Her emphasis on social media as a primary tool for communication and marketing demonstrated her ability to anticipate future trends in consumer behaviour and the rise of influencer marketing.

One of Weiss's most impressive strategic planning feats is navigating Glossier's rapid growth. Rather than rushing to scale, she carefully considered each new product launch, ensuring that every addition to the Glossier lineup fit within the company's brand ethos. This systematic approach to expansion and a clear long-term vision helped Glossier maintain its authenticity and deep connection with its customers, even as it became a significant player in the global beauty industry.

Emily Weiss's ability to turn a beauty blog into a global brand is a testament to the power of strategic planning. By focusing sharply on her vision—building a beauty brand for real people, driven by their needs and desires—she transformed Glossier into a disruptive force in the beauty world.

NAVIGATING THE WHY

One key benefit of strategic planning is its ability to foster alignment and coherence within your business. When everyone—from the leadership team to frontline employees—is aware of and committed to the strategic goals, the organisation operates more efficiently and effectively. This shared understanding and commitment create a unified effort toward common objectives, enhancing overall performance and fostering a sense of collective purpose.

Furthermore, strategic planning encourages continuous improvement and innovation. By regularly reviewing and refining strategies, you can stay ahead of industry trends and technological advancements. This iterative process ensures that your business remains agile and adaptable, capable of responding to market shifts and evolving customer needs. As you explore this chapter, you'll gain a deeper understanding of the critical role strategic planning plays in driving long-term success and learn practical steps to integrate this practice into your operations.

Cognitive and Psychological Foundations

One of strategic planning's primary benefits is its ability to reduce uncertainty. In a business context, uncertainty can lead to anxiety and impaired decision-making. Cognitive psychology research has shown that having a clear, well-defined plan can alleviate these adverse effects by providing a roadmap for the future. This structured approach allows leaders to anticipate potential challenges and opportunities, making more informed and confident decisions.

Strategic planning involves mental simulation, where you envision various future scenarios and plan accordingly. This mental rehearsal is similar to the concept of prospective hindsight used in pre-mortems. You and your team can prepare for multiple possibilities by imagining different outcomes and strategising responses. Being prepared strengthens resilience and adaptability, essential for navigating a dynamic business landscape.

Organisational Benefits

Regular strategic planning fosters alignment and coherence within your business. It ensures that all departments and employees work towards common goals, creating a unified effort that enhances overall efficiency and effectiveness. This alignment is crucial for maintaining focus and direction, especially during change or uncertainty. When everyone understands the company's strategic objectives and their role in achieving them, the organisation operates more smoothly and cohesively.

Studies consistently show that companies with robust strategic planning processes are more likely to successfully achieve their objectives and adapt to changing market conditions. Strategic planning encourages a proactive rather than reactive approach to business challenges, enabling you to stay ahead of industry trends and technological advancements. This forward-thinking mindset is essential for maintaining a competitive edge and driving sustained performance.

IT'S NOT ALL PLAIN SAILING

Strategic planning is a powerful tool, but the journey is rarely smooth. Obstacles like resistance to change, balancing competing priorities, and keeping plans relevant in a fast-moving world can hinder progress if not managed effectively. However, by anticipating these challenges and adopting proactive strategies, you can ensure your plan remains robust and adaptable. From gaining buy-in across your organisation to striking the right balance between long-term vision and short-term demands, overcoming these hurdles is essential for sustainable success.

Overcoming Resistance

One significant challenge in strategic planning is overcoming resistance from employees and stakeholders. This resistance can stem from various sources, including the perceived complexity of the planning process or fear of change. To address this, it's vital to communicate the benefits of strategic planning. Explain how a well-crafted strategic plan can increase efficiency, better resource allocation, and long-term success. Share success stories from other organisations to illustrate these tangible benefits.

Involving employees and stakeholders in the planning process can also help mitigate resistance. When people feel they have a voice in shaping the strategy, they are more likely to buy into the plan and support its implementation. Create open dialogue and feedback opportunities, ensuring everyone's concerns and ideas are considered. Workshops, brainstorming sessions, and collaborative planning meetings can foster a sense of ownership and commitment.

Balancing Long-Term and Short-Term Goals

Another common challenge is balancing long-term strategic goals with short-term operational needs. Focusing too much on immediate concerns can lead to neglecting long-term objectives, while an exclusive focus on the future can make it challenging to address pressing current issues.

Developing a flexible planning approach can help strike this balance. Start by setting clear long-term goals that define the company's direction and vision. These goals should be ambitious yet achievable, providing a roadmap for where you want to go.

Next, break down these long-term goals into smaller, actionable steps that can be integrated into daily operations. This approach ensures that immediate actions contribute to the broader strategy. Use frameworks like OKRs (Objectives and Key Results) to align short-term activities with long-term objectives.

Review and adjust your plans regularly to accommodate new information and changing circumstances. This iterative process allows you to stay on course while remaining agile and responsive to emerging opportunities and challenges.

Keeping Plans Relevant

The business environment constantly evolves, and strategic plans must be adaptable to remain effective. Keeping plans relevant in a dynamic landscape requires continuous monitoring and updating. Implement a system for regularly reviewing and updating your strategic plans. Schedule quarterly or bi-annual review sessions to assess progress and make necessary adjustments. During these reviews, evaluate the external environment using tools like PESTEL analysis to identify any political, economic, social, technological, environmental, or legal shifts that may impact your business.

Encourage a culture of continuous improvement within your organisation. This means being open to feedback, learning from successes and failures, and being willing to pivot when needed. Foster an environment where innovation is encouraged and new ideas are welcomed.

Empower yourself by staying informed about industry trends, technological advancements, and market dynamics. Participate in industry conferences, subscribe to relevant publications, and network with other professionals to stay updated on the latest developments. This knowledge will give you the confidence to anticipate changes and proactively adjust your strategic plans, putting you in control of your business journey.

YOUR ROUTE TO SUCCESS

Developing practical strategic planning skills is like charting a course for a long and unpredictable expedition. You need a clear vision, the right tools, and the ability to adapt to changing conditions.

Set Clear, Measurable Goals

Imagine embarking on a journey without a destination in mind. You might wander, unsure of where you're headed. Setting clear, measurable goals is your map and compass, guiding you towards your destination. To ensure these goals are practical, consider making them Personal, Positive, and in the Present Tense:

- **Personal:** Your goals should be meaningful to you and aligned with your values and aspirations. When a goal is personal, it resonates more deeply, increasing your motivation to achieve it. Reflect on what truly matters to you and how each goal fits your vision.

- **Positive:** Frame your goals positively. Instead of focusing on what you want to avoid, emphasise what you want to achieve. For instance, rather than saying, *"I want to stop missing deadlines,"* say, *"I meet all my deadlines consistently."* Positive framing boosts your morale and sets a constructive tone for your efforts.

- **Present Tense:** Write your goals as if they are already happening. This psychological trick helps internalise the goal and reinforces the belief that it is achievable. For example, instead of saying, *"I will become a confident speaker,"* say, *"I am a confident speaker."* This approach helps your mind align with the reality you are working towards.

Involve your team in setting these goals. Their insights and buy-in are invaluable, helping to refine the goals and ensuring everyone is on the same page. This collaborative approach fosters a sense of unity and shared vision, making the journey towards your goals a team effort.

Aligning Resources

Aligning your resources with your strategic goals ensures you have everything you need for the journey. Start by conducting a resource audit. Imagine checking your ship's supplies, crew skills, and condition before setting sail. Identify your strengths and gaps, ensuring you're well-prepared for the voyage ahead.

Next, prioritise your initiatives. Focus on the projects that will have the most significant impact on your journey. Allocate resources—whether it's time, financial reserves, or technology—where they're needed most. Develop a detailed plan that outlines how resources will be used. This aspiration should be flexible, allowing you to reallocate resources as priorities change or new opportunities arise.

Continuous Assessment

Regularly checking your course and adjusting as you navigate the seas is essential. Continuous assessment ensures you stay on track and can adapt to changing conditions. Establish regular review cycles, like scheduled stops at ports along your route. These reviews allow you to evaluate your progress and make necessary adjustments. Use tools like SWOT analysis to assess your strengths, weaknesses, opportunities, threats, and PESTEL analysis to understand the broader environment.

Gather feedback from your team and other stakeholders. Their insights can provide valuable perspectives and help you uncover blind spots. Track key performance indicators (KPIs) to measure your success and identify areas needing attention. Treat strategic planning as an iterative process. Much like a seasoned navigator who constantly adjusts the sails and course based on the weather and sea conditions, continuously refine your plans to stay aligned with your goals.

Developing Strategic Planning

Enhance your strategic planning skills by seeking continuous learning opportunities. Attend workshops and seminars to learn from experts and peers, gain hands-on experience, and network— Enrol in online courses and certifications to deepen your understanding and stay updated on best practices.

Seek mentorship from experienced strategists or business leaders. Their guidance can provide invaluable insights, like a professional sea captain mentoring a new navigator. By setting clear goals, aligning resources, and continuously assessing and refining your plans, you can navigate the complexities of your business landscape with confidence and precision.

INSIGHTS FROM MY JOURNEY

Throughout my career, I've had the privilege of seeing many brands launch or reinvent themselves. One thing that stands out about those that have endured is their commitment to regularly revising their strategic plans. While it's common for businesses to complete a three-year strategic plan and then leave it untouched, the brands that have truly stood the test of time are the ones that revisit and refine their plans every year.

A strategic plan isn't something you create once and file away—it's a living document that needs constant attention. I've consistently seen successful businesses that take the time to review their long-term goals, assess progress, and make adjustments based on the current environment. This proactive approach allows them to stay competitive, adapt to new challenges, and seize emerging opportunities.

24. BUILDING YOUR CREW

People are the heartbeat that drives growth, innovation, and resilience. Your team's talent and dedication can determine your company's path, making human resource management a crucial part of your strategic planning. Focusing on people ensures you attract top talent and retain and nurture these individuals, creating an environment where innovation and productivity can flourish.

In a world where technology and market dynamics constantly evolve, strategic people management is more critical than ever. By prioritising your employees' needs and development, you boost their productivity and engagement and build a resilient and adaptive organisation. Employees are not just workers; they are crucial stakeholders whose satisfaction and wellbeing directly impact your business outcomes. Companies that excel at empowering their people often outperform their peers, enjoying higher levels of employee engagement, lower turnover rates, and superior customer satisfaction.

LEADING THE WAY

Since its inception in 2006, Shopify has grown into one of the world's leading e-commerce platforms, empowering over a million businesses worldwide. Much of this success can be attributed to CEO Tobi Lütke's unique leadership and team-building approach, which prioritises a strong company culture and fosters an environment of creativity, autonomy, and continuous learning.

Empowering Teams Through Autonomy and Trust

Lütke's leadership philosophy centres around empowering his employees by giving them autonomy and trust. He believes the best ideas often come from individuals and teams free to innovate without micromanagement. Rather than enforcing a rigid hierarchy, Shopify encourages employees at all levels to contribute ideas and take ownership of their work.

For Lütke, building a great product like Shopify isn't about having the best individual contributors but creating an environment where people can collectively thrive. By allowing his team to experiment, make mistakes, and learn, Lütke has fostered a culture of innovation. This freedom has led to groundbreaking features that have kept Shopify ahead of its competitors.

Focus on Continuous Learning

Another critical element of Lütke's leadership is his belief in continuous learning and development. Shopify invests heavily in its employees, offering opportunities for growth, professional development, and cross-team collaboration. Lütke understands that investing in his people is not just good for them; it's good for the business. By providing access to learning resources and encouraging knowledge-sharing across teams, Shopify ensures its workforce remains adaptable and ahead of the curve in a rapidly evolving tech landscape.

Lütke also embodies this ethos of lifelong learning himself, regularly engaging with books, online courses, and the latest technology trends. This commitment to growth, personally and within his team, has helped Shopify stay agile in a constantly changing industry.

Building Behaviours

Under Lütke's leadership, Shopify has cultivated a resilient and adaptable workforce. During challenging times, such as the COVID-19 pandemic, Shopify's ability to quickly pivot to support businesses transitioning online was a testament to the strength and flexibility of its team. Lütke's forward-thinking decision to transition Shopify into a remote-first company during the pandemic exemplifies how he prioritises the wellbeing and productivity of his people while adapting to external circumstances.

Tobias Lütke demonstrates how building the right team and investing in their growth can lead to extraordinary business success by focusing on team empowerment, continuous learning, and fostering a culture of innovation. His leadership at Shopify shows that a people-first approach creates the foundation for an organisation that thrives, even in times of uncertainty.

NAVIGATING THE WHY

Effective people management is not just about strategies and tactics but also about understanding the psychological, organisational behaviour, and human resources principles that underpin it. These foundations provide the insights we need to motivate, engage, and retain employees, enhancing overall organisational performance.

Psychological Foundations

Understanding what drives human behaviour is a cornerstone of effective people management. Theories like Maslow's *Hierarchy of Needs* offer valuable insights into the motivations of individuals at different levels. According to Maslow, once basic physiological and safety needs are met, individuals seek to fulfil higher-level needs such as belonging, esteem, and self-actualisation. Creating workplace environments that cater to these needs can significantly enhance employee satisfaction and performance.

Another critical theory is Herzberg's *Two-Factor Theory*, which distinguishes between hygiene factors (salary and job security) and motivators (recognition and personal growth). While hygiene factors prevent dissatisfaction, motivators drive engagement and satisfaction. Understanding and applying these theories can help managers create more fulfilling work experiences.

Organisational Behaviour

Research in organisational behaviour highlights the importance of social dynamics and workplace culture in employee performance. Studies show that a positive organisational culture, characterised by trust, collaboration, and open communication, significantly boosts employee morale and productivity. The social identity theory suggests that employees who strongly identify with their organisation are more likely to be committed and motivated.

Another crucial element is the concept of psychological safety, popularised by Harvard professor Amy Edmondson. Psychological safety refers to the belief that one can speak up, share ideas, and take risks without fear of negative consequences. Teams that foster psychological safety are more innovative, resilient, and effective.

Impact of Employee Engagement

Employee engagement is a critical factor in business success. Engaged employees are emotionally invested in their work and the organisation, leading to higher productivity, lower absenteeism, and more excellent retention. Research from Gallup shows that businesses with high engagement levels outperform their peers in profitability, productivity, and customer satisfaction.

Neuroscience and Motivation

Recent advances in neuroscience provide deeper insights into motivating and engaging employees. Studies on the brain's reward system show that recognition and positive reinforcement trigger the release of dopamine, a neurotransmitter associated with pleasure and motivation. This underscores the importance of regular feedback and recognition in maintaining high employee motivation.

Diversity and Inclusion

Diverse and inclusive workplaces are ethically essential and drive business success. Research from McKinsey & Company shows that companies with diverse workforces are more likely to outperform their peers in profitability. Diversity brings different perspectives and ideas, fostering creativity and innovation. Inclusion ensures that all employees feel valued and able to contribute fully, leading to higher engagement and retention.

Strategic People Practices

Strategic people management integrates human resource practices with the overall business strategy. This involves aligning recruitment, training, performance management, and employee development with the company's goals. Effective strategic HR practices ensure the organisation has the right talent to achieve its objectives and adapt to changing market conditions.

IT'S NOT ALL PLAIN SAILING

Implementing people-centric strategies is essential for fostering a thriving workplace, but the journey is not without its challenges. From overcoming resistance to change to balancing immediate pressures with long-term goals, organisations must navigate several obstacles to ensure success. Addressing these challenges head-on—through clear communication, consistent leadership alignment, and a commitment to continuous improvement—can significantly enhance employee engagement, satisfaction, and overall performance.

Resistance to Change

Resistance to change is a significant barrier when implementing new strategies. Communicating the benefits of people-centric initiatives, involving employees in the change process, and providing adequate training and support can help overcome this resistance.

- **Cultural Resistance:** Employees and leaders may resist changes to traditional practices and mindsets. Overcoming this resistance requires effective communication about the benefits of people-centric strategies and involving employees in the change process. Provide training and resources to help them adapt to new approaches.
- **Change Management:** Implementing people-centric strategies often involves significant organisational change. Develop a comprehensive change management plan with clear communication, stakeholder engagement, and support mechanisms to help employees navigate the transition.

Balancing Short-Term and Long-Term Goals

Balancing immediate pressures with long-term people-centric initiatives can be complex. Demonstrating how these initiatives contribute to short-term and long-term success and integrating them into strategic planning can help strike this balance.

- **Immediate Pressures:** Organisations may face pressure to deliver short-term results, challenging investing in long-term people-centric initiatives. Strike a balance by demonstrating how these initiatives can contribute to immediate and future success. Highlight quick wins that showcase the benefits of people-centric strategies.
- **Resource Allocation:** When competing priorities exist, allocating resources to people-centric initiatives can be complex. Ensure that your strategic planning process focuses on long-term people development and integrates it with other business goals.

Maintaining Consistency

Implementing people-centric strategies consistently across departments and teams requires standardised policies and practices. Aligning leadership with these strategies and regularly reviewing implementation consistency is crucial for success.

- **Consistency in Implementation:** Ensuring consistent implementation of people-centric strategies across different departments and teams can be challenging. However, with regular review and assessment, you can stay proactive and in control. Develop standardised policies and practices that are flexible enough to be adapted to specific contexts. Regularly review and assess the consistency of implementation.
- **Leadership Alignment:** Aligning leadership at all levels with people-centric strategies is crucial for success. Provide training and development for leaders to understand and embody these principles. Foster a culture of accountability where leaders are responsible for promoting and maintaining a people-centric approach.

Measuring Impact

Measuring the impact of people-centric strategies can be challenging, particularly for soft metrics like employee engagement and wellbeing. Combining quantitative and qualitative methods and investing in HR technology and data analytics can help assess effectiveness.

- **Quantifying Soft Metrics:** Measuring the impact of people-centric strategies on metrics like employee engagement, satisfaction, and wellbeing can be difficult. Use a combination of quantitative and qualitative methods to assess the effectiveness of your initiatives. Employee surveys, feedback sessions, and focus groups can provide valuable insights.

- **Data Collection and Analysis:** Collecting and analysing data on people-centric initiatives requires robust systems and processes. Investing in HR technology and data analytics tools is crucial, it's a game-changer. This investment will equip you with the necessary insights to continuously improve your strategies, making you feel confident and prepared for the future.

Sustaining Momentum

Sustaining people-centric strategies requires a long-term commitment and continuous improvement. Embedding these principles into organisational culture and strategic planning and regularly reviewing and adjusting plans based on feedback ensure ongoing success.

- **Long-Term Commitment:** Sustaining people-centric strategies requires ongoing commitment from leadership and the entire organisation. Avoid treating these initiatives as one-time projects. Embed people-centric principles into the organisational culture and strategic planning process.

- **Continuous Improvement:** Committing to continuous improvement is critical to sustaining people-centric strategies. Regularly review your plan to reflect changing organisational needs and external factors. Foster a culture where feedback is valued and adjustments are made based on lessons learned, ensuring your strategies remain practical and relevant.

Navigating Diversity and Inclusion

Creating a diverse and inclusive workplace fosters innovation, engagement, and a sense of belonging among employees. This involves addressing unconscious biases and developing inclusive practices that go beyond compliance. Promoting diversity, equity, and inclusion (DEI) can build a more vital, dynamic organisation.

- **Overcoming Bias:** Addressing unconscious bias and fostering a truly inclusive environment can be challenging. Provide training on DEI to help employees recognise and mitigate bias. Implement policies and practices that promote fairness and equal opportunities.

- **Inclusive Practices:** True inclusivity requires continuous engagement with diverse groups within your organisation. Understanding their experiences and needs allows you to develop practices that foster a genuine sense of belonging for all employees.

Managing Remote and Hybrid Work

The shift to remote and hybrid work models challenges communication, collaboration, and work-life balance. Effectively managing these challenges involves investing in the right technologies and developing supportive policies. Doing so ensures that your team remains connected, productive, and engaged, regardless of their physical location.

- **Communication and Collaboration:** Facilitating effective communication and collaboration in remote and hybrid work environments requires the right technology and tools. Investing in these resources helps maintain strong connections among team members and ensures seamless partnership.
- **Work-Life Integration:** Supporting work-life balance in remote and hybrid work environments can be complex. Develop policies that promote flexibility while setting clear expectations. Provide resources for remote work, including ergonomic equipment and mental health support.

YOUR ROUTE TO SUCCESS

Developing people-centric strategies creates an environment where employees feel valued, engaged, and empowered to contribute to your organisation's success. This holistic approach covers various aspects of human resource management, leadership, and organisational culture. You can build a thriving business that drives success and innovation by fostering a positive work environment, investing in professional development, and promoting diversity and inclusion.

Foster a Positive Work Environment

Creating a supportive culture and promoting work-life balance are foundational to a positive work environment. Encouraging open communication, recognising diverse perspectives, and providing mental health resources can significantly enhance employee satisfaction and productivity.

- **Create a Supportive Culture:** Cultivate a workplace culture prioritising respect, collaboration, and inclusivity. Encourage open communication and allow employees to share their ideas and feedback. Recognise and celebrate diverse perspectives to foster a sense of belonging.
- **Promote Work-Life Balance:** Implement policies that support work-life balance, such as flexible work schedules, remote work options, and paid time off. Providing mental health and wellbeing resources, such as access to counselling services and wellness programs, can also enhance employee satisfaction and productivity.

Invest in Professional Development

Investing in continuous learning and leadership development is crucial for empowering your employees to grow and succeed. Offering training programs, mentorship opportunities, and cross-functional projects can help your team acquire new skills and advance their careers.

- **Continuous Learning Opportunities:** Offer training and development programs to help employees acquire new skills and advance their careers. This can include workshops, online courses, mentorship programs, and opportunities for cross-functional projects.
- **Leadership Development:** Develop programs that identify and nurture future leaders within the organisation. Provide training on essential leadership skills, such as emotional intelligence, conflict resolution, and strategic thinking. Encourage leaders to mentor and support their teams.

Implement Effective Performance Management

Effective performance management involves setting clear expectations, providing regular feedback, and utilising data-driven decisions. Recognising and rewarding achievements can motivate and retain top talent, while performance management software can streamline processes and provide valuable insights.

- **Clear Expectations and Feedback:** Set performance expectations and provide regular employee feedback. Use performance reviews to discuss career goals, strengths, and areas for improvement. Recognise and reward achievements to motivate and retain top talent.

- **Data-Driven Decision Making:** Utilise data and analytics to assess employee performance and identify trends. This can help you make informed decisions about promotions, compensation, and personal development. Performance management software can streamline this process and provide valuable insights.

Enhance Employee Engagement and Retention

Developing employee recognition programs and creating clear career pathways can significantly boost engagement and retention. Personalised recognition and a roadmap for advancement help motivate employees and reduce turnover.

- **Employee Recognition Programs:** Develop programs that recognise and reward employee contributions. This can include awards, bonuses, and public praise. Personalised recognition, such as handwritten notes or small gifts, can also significantly impact.

- **Career Pathways:** Create clear career pathways that outline potential growth opportunities within the business. Providing a roadmap for advancement can increase employee motivation and reduce turnover. Offer resources and support to help employees achieve their career goals.

Promote Diversity, Equity, and Inclusion (DEI)

Promoting DEI through inclusive hiring practices and equitable opportunities is essential for a thriving organisational culture. Implementing policies that eliminate biases and supporting employee resource groups can foster a sense of belonging for all team members.

- **Inclusive Hiring Practices:** Implement hiring practices that promote diversity and eliminate biases. This can include diverse interview panels, anonymous resume reviews, and outreach to underrepresented groups. Ensure that job descriptions and recruitment materials reflect the organisation's commitment to DEI.

- **Equitable Opportunities:** Provide equitable access to opportunities for all employees, regardless of their background. This can include equal pay for equal work, accessible professional development programs, and support for employee resource groups (ERGs).

Leverage Technology

People management software, systems, and data analytics can streamline processes, enhance communication, and provide valuable insights into employee engagement and performance. Investing in these tools can support the implementation of people-centric strategies.

- **Technology Solutions:** Invest in technology solutions, such as human resource information systems (HRIS), learning management systems (LMS), and employee engagement platforms. These tools can streamline HR processes, enhance communication, and provide valuable insights into employee engagement and performance.

- **Data Analytics:** Use data analytics to identify trends and patterns in employee behaviour, engagement, and performance. This can help you make informed decisions about HR strategies and interventions. Regularly review and analyse data to assess the effectiveness of your people-centric initiatives.

Encourage Innovation and Creativity

Encouraging innovation and creativity involves developing programs that foster a safe space for experimentation and recognise innovative thinking. Providing resources and support for new ideas can drive continuous improvement and growth.

- **Innovation Programs:** Develop programs that encourage innovation and creativity among employees. This can include hackathons, innovation labs, and suggestion programs. Provide resources and support for employees to experiment with new ideas and approaches.
- **Safe Space for Experimentation:** Create a safe environment where employees feel comfortable taking risks and experimenting with new ideas. Encourage a mindset of continuous improvement and learning from failure. Recognise and reward innovative thinking and problem-solving.

Regular Reviews and Updates

Regularly reviewing and updating your people-centric strategies is crucial for continuous improvement. Establishing clear performance metrics, implementing feedback mechanisms, and conducting quarterly reviews ensure your initiatives remain effective and aligned with organisational goals.

- **Performance Metrics:** Establish clear performance metrics to evaluate the effectiveness of your people-centric strategies. Regularly review these metrics to identify areas for improvement and track progress. Metrics might include employee engagement scores, retention rates, productivity levels, and customer satisfaction.
- **Feedback Mechanisms:** Implement regular feedback loops where employees can share their experiences and provide input on people-centric initiatives. Use surveys, focus groups, and one-on-one meetings to gather diverse perspectives. Act on the feedback received to make continuous improvements.
- **Quarterly Reviews:** Schedule quarterly reviews of your people-centric strategies to ensure they align with organisational goals and market conditions. These reviews should include leadership, HR, and key stakeholders to discuss progress, challenges, and necessary adjustments.

INSIGHTS FROM MY JOURNEY

One of the most important lessons I've learned throughout my career is that success is rarely achieved alone. Many of the achievements I'm most proud of have been delivered by the team around me. Whether it was in a corporate environment or my own business, I've always relied on the strengths, perspectives, and efforts of others to drive success.

As I transitioned into running my own business, I realised that surrounding yourself with talented individuals who bring diverse skills and viewpoints improves the quality of work and enhances problem-solving and innovation. No single person has all the answers, and it's often through the collective intelligence of a team that the best solutions emerge. I've found that creating an environment where people feel valued, respected, and empowered ignites a sense of ownership and motivation that leads to exceptional results.

Moreover, the relationships you build—with internal employees or external partners—are the bedrock of your business's resilience and adaptability. When you foster trust and respect within your network, you create a support system enabling you to approach challenges confidently. This network helps you navigate difficult times and accelerates growth by opening up new opportunities for collaboration, innovation, and shared success.

I've seen firsthand how a people-first mindset can transform a business. When individuals feel invested in the outcomes, the culture shifts from mere task completion to one where everyone works toward a common goal. The sense of collective achievement boosts morale and engagement, ensuring that success is shared, celebrated, and sustainable. Ultimately, the people around you make the difference in business. The right team can elevate your vision, push boundaries, and achieve what might seem impossible alone.

25. STREAMLINING THE JOURNEY

Aligning all areas of your business ensures that every department works towards common goals, reducing inefficiencies and boosting overall performance. When your people strategies align with your operational objectives and financial practices support your marketing efforts, you create a synergistic company where every part enhances the other. This unity fosters a sense of purpose among employees, keeping them motivated and engaged.

Strategic growth isn't just about expanding your market share or increasing revenues; it's about sustainable development that aligns with your core values and long-term goals. Integrating best practices across all business functions builds a solid foundation for this growth. For example, when marketing strategies are based on thorough market research and align with the company's strategic goals, they attract and retain the right customers, driving long-term success.

LEADING THE WAY

Julian Hearn, the founder of Huel, set out in 2015 with a bold vision: to create nutritionally complete, convenient food that supports sustainability. The result was Huel, a complete food brand that provides a balanced mix of protein, carbohydrates, fats, and all essential vitamins and minerals. Huel has since grown into a global sensation, and its success is deeply rooted in its commitment to continuous improvement.

Revolutionising Nutrition

Hearn's mission was clear from the outset: to make nutritionally complete food that is healthy, sustainable, and accessible. However, the journey to perfecting Huel's products has been a constant process of refinement, guided by customer feedback, scientific research, and evolving market demands. The company regularly revises its product formulations, using customer suggestions and insights from nutrition experts to ensure that every iteration meets high taste, texture, and nutritional value standards.

Iterative Product Development

One of the critical drivers of Huel's success has been its ability to improve continuously. Initially launched as a powdered meal replacement, Huel's product line has since expanded to include ready-to-drink shakes, bars, and hot meals, all developed in response to consumer demand. Each new product goes through rigorous development cycles, where feedback from customers and employees is gathered and analysed to inform product updates. This iterative process ensures that Huel stays ahead of competitors and remains aligned with its mission of offering healthy, sustainable, and affordable food.

Sustainability and Efficiency

Julian Hearn's focus on sustainability extends beyond the products themselves. Huel constantly refines its packaging to minimise waste and reduce its environmental footprint, aligning with its sustainability ethos. In addition, the company applies lean business principles to streamline operations, ensuring that every aspect of the supply chain is efficient. From production to distribution, Huel optimises processes to reduce costs while maintaining high product quality, creating a business model prioritising profit and purpose.

Customer-Centric Innovation

Huel's journey exemplifies how continuous improvement, driven by customer feedback and scientific research, can create an enduring brand that responds to market trends and helps shape them. Huel and Julian Hearn have demonstrated the power of aligning business strategy with customer needs and environmental responsibility by fostering a culture of innovation and constantly seeking ways to improve its offerings.

Huel's success story highlights how a commitment to continuous improvement and strategic alignment across all functions—product development, customer engagement, and sustainability—can drive innovation and create a lasting impact in an increasingly competitive market.

NAVIGATING THE WHY

The principles of holistic business management are rooted in cognitive psychology and organisational theory. This approach emphasises the importance of alignment and coherence across all business functions, ensuring that every part of the organisation works harmoniously towards common objectives.

Cognitive and Psychological Foundations

Organisational cohesion is crucial for business success. Studies in organisational psychology show that companies with aligned practices perform better and adapt more effectively to changes. This cohesion reduces silos, enhances communication, and ensures that all parts of the organisation work towards common goals. When departments are aligned, they share information more freely, collaborate more effectively, and support each other's efforts, leading to a more unified and productive work environment.

Systems thinking is a critical concept in organisational theory that highlights the interconnectedness of different business functions. This approach views the business as an integrated system where each part influences and is influenced by others. By adopting a systems thinking perspective, you can better understand how changes in one area impact others. This holistic view enables more informed decision-making as it considers the broader implications of actions and policies across the organisation. For instance, a change in the production process may affect supply chain management, sales, and customer service, requiring coordinated adjustments to maintain overall efficiency.

Impact on Business Performance

Research indicates that businesses adopting holistic management practices experience higher productivity. When all functions are aligned and working towards common goals, there is less duplication of efforts and fewer inefficiencies. This streamlined approach ensures that resources are used effectively, and employees can focus on high-value tasks that drive the organisation forward. For example, a holistic approach to project management ensures that all departments involved in a project are coordinated, reducing delays and improving overall outcomes.

Employee engagement is significantly enhanced in companies that embrace holistic management. When employees see that their work contributes to a larger purpose and that there is alignment between their roles and the organisation's goals, they are more likely to be motivated and committed. This sense of purpose fosters a positive work environment, increases job satisfaction, and reduces turnover rates. Holistic management practices often include continuous feedback and development opportunities, which further engage and retain employees.

Aligning principles and processes across all functions leads to more consistent and effective strategy execution, directly impacting customer satisfaction. A holistic approach ensures that every touchpoint with the customer, from marketing and sales to delivery and after-sales service, aligns with the company's values and objectives. This consistency builds trust and loyalty as customers experience seamless and reliable service. For example, a company that aligns its marketing messages with product development and customer service processes provides a more cohesive and satisfying customer experience.

IT'S NOT ALL PLAIN SAILING

Adopting a holistic approach to business management can transform your organisation, but it's not without its hurdles. Successfully integrating new principles, practices, and processes across departments requires careful planning, clear communication, and a culture that embraces change. From overcoming resistance to managing the complexities of integration, a holistic approach calls for a proactive strategy that aligns everyone with the organisation's values and objectives. By tackling these challenges head-on, you can create a cohesive and adaptable business environment that drives sustainable success.

Resistance to Change

Resistance to change is a significant barrier when implementing new principles, practices, and processes across an organisation.

Employees and managers may hesitate to alter established routines and fear the uncertainty of change.

- **Involving Stakeholders:** From the beginning, employees and managers are involved in the planning and implementation. This will help them understand the reasons for change, how it will benefit the organisation, and their roles in the new system.
- **Clear Communication:** Communicate the benefits of the new practices and how they align with the company's goals and values. Use multiple channels—meetings, emails, workshops—to ensure everyone is informed and engaged.
- **Training and Support:** Provide adequate training and support to help employees adapt to new systems and processes. This can reduce anxiety and build confidence in their ability to succeed in the new environment.

Complexity of Integration

Integrating practices and processes across different functions can be highly complex. Each department may have unique workflows, tools, and priorities that must be harmonised.

- **Project Management Tools:** Use project management tools and methodologies, such as Agile or Lean, to manage the integration process. These tools can help organise tasks, timelines, and responsibilities, making the integration more manageable.
- **Cross-Functional Teams:** Establish cross-functional teams to facilitate department communication and collaboration. These teams can identify potential conflicts and work together to develop integrated solutions.
- **Phased Implementation:** Consider a phased approach to integration. Implement changes gradually, allowing time for

each phase to be absorbed and stabilised before moving on to the next. This reduces the risk of overwhelming the organisation and allows for adjustments based on feedback.

Maintaining Alignment

Ensuring that all functions remain aligned with the organisation's core values and strategic objectives requires continuous effort. Misalignment can lead to inefficiencies and conflicting priorities.

- **Regular Reviews:** Regularly review practices and processes to ensure they align with the company's strategic goals. Use these reviews to identify areas of misalignment and make necessary adjustments.
- **Continuous Communication:** Maintain open lines of communication across all levels of the organisation. Regular updates from leadership on strategic priorities and progress can help keep everyone focused and aligned.
- **Performance Metrics:** Develop performance metrics that align with core values and strategic objectives. Regularly measure and report on these metrics to ensure that all departments contribute to the organisation's overall goals.

Creating a Culture of Adaptability

A culture that embraces change and adaptability can significantly reduce resistance and facilitate smoother integration of new practices.

- **Leadership Role:** As a leader, your behaviour sets the tone for the rest of the business. Ensure you lead by example and model adaptability and openness to change

- **Encouraging Innovation:** Allow employees to test new ideas and approaches, fostering a culture where change is seen as an opportunity rather than a threat.

YOUR ROUTE TO SUCCESS

Developing holistic business practices involves creating a cohesive framework that integrates principles, practices, and processes across all functions of your organisation. This approach ensures that every department operates harmoniously, contributing to your business's strategic goals and values.

Define Core Values and Principles

To lay a strong foundation for holistic business practices, clearly define the core values and principles that will guide your organisation. These values should reflect your company's mission and vision, setting the tone for the culture and decision-making processes throughout the business.

- **Articulation of Values:** Engage leadership and key stakeholders in a values-defining exercise. Identify the fundamental principles that embody your business ethos and ensure these values are documented and communicated across all levels of the organisation.
- **Embedding Values:** Integrate these values into the organisational culture through training programs, performance metrics, and recognition systems. Ensure that every employee understands and aligns with these core values.
- **Leadership Example:** You should exemplify these values in your actions and decisions, setting a standard for the rest of

the business. Consistent behaviour from the top reinforces the importance of these principles.

Align Practices Across Functions

Ensuring alignment across various business functions is crucial for maintaining organisational coherence and synergy. This alignment can be achieved through structured practices that foster collaboration and standardisation.

- **Cross-Functional Teams:** Establish cross-functional teams to work on strategic projects. Include members from different departments to encourage diverse perspectives and integrated solutions.
- **Standardised Processes:** Develop standardised processes that can be applied across departments—document standard operating procedures (SOPs) and best practices to ensure consistency in operations.
- **Regular Communication:** Implement regular communication channels such as interdepartmental meetings, newsletters, and collaborative platforms. This ensures that all departments are aware of each other's activities, fostering a collaborative environment and reducing the risk of people working in silos.

Implement Integrated Processes

Integrated process management is essential for streamlining workflows and ensuring consistency across your organisation. Leveraging technology and structured methodologies can facilitate this integration.

- **Enterprise Resource Planning (ERP) Systems:** Invest in ERP systems that integrate various business processes into a unified platform. ERP systems can connect finance, HR, supply chain, and other functions, providing real-time data and improving operational efficiency.

- **Process Mapping:** Conduct process mapping exercises to visualise and analyse current workflows. Identify areas of overlap, inefficiency, and disconnect, and redesign processes to enhance integration and streamline operations.
- **Continuous Improvement:** Establish a continuous improvement framework such as Lean or Six Sigma. Encourage employees to identify and suggest workflow improvements and implement these suggestions to keep processes dynamic and efficient.

Utilise Data Analytics

Data-driven decision-making is a cornerstone of holistic business practices. Implement data analytics tools to gather insights across all business functions.

- **KPI Tracking:** Develop each department's key performance indicators (KPIs) and use data analytics to track these metrics. Review performance data regularly to identify trends, strengths, and areas for improvement.
- **Predictive Analytics:** Use predictive analytics to anticipate market trends, customer behaviour, and operational challenges. This proactive approach lets you make informed strategic decisions and stay ahead of the competition.

Foster Learning

Creating a continuous learning environment is crucial for maintaining a holistic approach to business management.

- **Training and Development:** Invest in continuous training and development programs for employees at all levels. This enhances individual skills and ensures the organisation adapts to new challenges and opportunities.

- **Knowledge Sharing:** Promote a knowledge-sharing culture through workshops, seminars, and internal databases. Encourage employees to share insights and best practices across departments.

Enhance Customer-Centric Practices

Integrating customer-centric practices across all functions ensures your organisation consistently delivers customer value.

- **Customer Feedback Loops:** Implement robust customer feedback mechanisms. Use this feedback to refine products, services, and processes, meeting customer needs and expectations.

- **Customer Journey Mapping:** Develop customer journey maps to understand the customer experience. Align internal processes to enhance interactions and satisfaction at every consumer touchpoint.

INSIGHTS FROM MY JOURNEY

Continuous improvement has always been a critical focus, whether developing a new product or service or simply refining how I work. I'm constantly looking for new ways to enhance the processes and practices I adopt, ensuring they are consistent across all business areas. This approach allows me to create a more cohesive and effective environment that strives to improve.

When approaching a new project, I don't just focus on the immediate task—I look at the bigger picture. I consider everything from the right hosting platform to the marketing strategy and, most importantly, the value it will bring to customers. By adopting a holistic mindset, I ensure that every aspect of the business is aligned and working toward the same goals.

Continuous improvement isn't just about fine-tuning processes—it's about ensuring every part of the business is connected and pulling in the same direction. When I approach projects this way, I've found that they become more successful, resilient, and adaptable. The more streamlined and consistent the approach, the greater the chance of long-term success.

26. CHARTING EXCEPTIONAL EXPERIENCES

Putting your customers at the heart of your business strategy is more critical than ever. A customer-centric approach isn't just about satisfying customers; it's about building long-term loyalty, fostering trust, and driving sustainable growth. True customer-centricity goes far beyond providing excellent service—it's about making the customer's needs and desires the core of every decision your business makes. Whether it's product development, marketing strategies, sales processes, or after-sales support, embedding the customer's perspective ensures that your business is always one step ahead in delivering value. By doing this, you don't just create satisfied customers—you create passionate advocates who drive word-of-mouth marketing and fuel your long-term success. Let's explore how to put the customer at the heart of your strategy and turn them into loyal ambassadors for your brand.

LEADING THE WAY

Founded in 2008 by Brian Chesky, Joe Gebbia, and Nathan Blecharczyk, Airbnb revolutionised the hospitality industry by creating a platform that connects travellers with unique accommodation experiences worldwide. What started as a small startup offering air mattresses in a living room has grown into a global brand, providing millions of people with diverse, personalised lodging experiences.

Transforming Hospitality

Airbnb's success lies in its commitment to customer-centricity and its focus on delivering exceptional experiences for guests and hosts. Unlike traditional hotels, Airbnb allows travellers to experience local culture, stay in unique homes, and engage directly with hosts, offering a level of personalisation and authenticity that standard accommodation often lacks. This approach has built trust and a loyal customer base, helping Airbnb grow from a niche idea to a mainstream global platform.

Airbnb understood from the outset that trust and safety were essential for building its community. To achieve this, the company implemented a robust review system where hosts and guests can rate and review each other, creating transparency and accountability. This mutual trust, enhanced by detailed profiles, identity verification, and clear communication, ensures that every guest and host feels secure and valued. This focus on transparency has been instrumental in establishing Airbnb's reputation as a reliable platform where travellers feel confident booking unique accommodations.

Personalised Experiences at Scale

One of Airbnb's key innovations was its ability to offer personalised experiences at scale. The platform continuously refines its services by leveraging data and customer feedback to match users' preferences and needs. Whether through curated travel suggestions, personalised recommendations, or tailored support, Airbnb consistently puts the customer at the heart of its business decisions.

Airbnb's agility and customer focus were further demonstrated during the 2020 pandemic when the travel industry faced unprecedented challenges. Instead of retreating, Airbnb offered *Online Experiences*, allowing hosts to share their expertise virtually. This innovative move enabled the company to continue supporting its community of hosts while offering guests unique, interactive experiences from the safety of their homes. It reinforced Airbnb's commitment to creating value for its users, even in the most challenging circumstances.

Empowering Hosts and Guests

For Airbnb, customer-centricity isn't just about the guest experience; it's also about empowering hosts. By providing a platform that allows hosts to generate income, showcase their homes, and offer personalised hospitality, Airbnb built a community where both sides benefit. The company's user-friendly tools and resources enable hosts to manage bookings, communicate effectively with guests, and maintain high service standards.

NAVIGATING THE WHY

Extensive research in psychology, marketing, and business management backs up the importance of customer-centricity. Understanding the science behind this approach can help you implement more effective strategies.

Customer Satisfaction and Loyalty

Studies show that businesses prioritising customer satisfaction enjoy higher customer loyalty. Satisfied customers are likelier to repeat purchases and recommend your company to others. This loyalty translates into long-term profitability and market stability.

For example, research from the Harvard Business Review indicates that increasing customer retention rates by just 5% can boost profits anywhere between 25% to 95%. This highlights the critical role of customer satisfaction in sustaining business growth.

Emotional Connections

Research in consumer psychology highlights the importance of emotional connections in building customer loyalty. Customers who feel an emotional connection with a brand are likelier to stay loyal, even in the face of competition. Creating positive emotional experiences can significantly impact customer retention and advocacy. A study by Capgemini found that customers with strong emotional connections to a brand have a 306% higher lifetime value. This underscores the power of emotional engagement in fostering deep, lasting relationships with customers.

Data-Driven Insights

Data analytics enables businesses to gain deeper insights into customer behaviours and preferences. By leveraging customer data, you can personalise your offerings, predict future needs, and tailor your marketing strategies to enhance customer satisfaction. Tools like Customer Relationship Management (CRM) systems, predictive analytics, and machine learning algorithms help you analyse vast customer data. This analysis helps identify trends, segment customers more effectively, and create targeted marketing campaigns that resonate with specific groups. For example, Netflix's recommendation algorithm uses data-driven insights to suggest content, significantly enhancing user experience and driving customer retention.

Behavioural Economics

Behavioural economics explores how psychological, cognitive, emotional, cultural, and social factors affect economic decisions. You can apply principles from behavioural economics to understand and influence customer behaviour. Techniques like framing (presenting information in a way that influences decision-making), anchoring (using initial information as a reference point for subsequent decisions), and social proof (leveraging customer reviews and testimonials) can enhance customer engagement and drive purchasing decisions.

Neuromarketing

Neuromarketing studies how the brain responds to marketing stimuli. By understanding the neural mechanisms behind customer decision-making, you can create more effective marketing strategies. Tools like eye-tracking, electroencephalography (EEG), and functional magnetic resonance imaging (fMRI) provide insights into how customers perceive and react to marketing messages, helping you design campaigns that capture attention and evoke desired emotional responses.

IT'S NOT ALL PLAIN SAILING

Shifting to a customer-centric business model is undeniably beneficial, but it comes with its own set of challenges. Successfully adopting this strategy requires overcoming internal resistance, aligning business objectives with customer needs, and ensuring everyone is equipped to deliver exceptional experiences. By fostering a clear understanding of the benefits, engaging employees at all levels, and integrating customer-centric initiatives into the broader business strategy, you can create a seamless transition.

Overcoming Resistance

Transitioning to a customer-centric approach often encounters resistance from employees and managers due to established habits, fear of change, and uncertainty about new methods.

- **Communicate the Benefits:** Clearly articulate the advantages of a customer-centric approach, such as increased customer loyalty, higher retention rates, and improved market positioning. Highlight success stories from other companies that have successfully made the transition.

- **Involve Employees:** Engage employees at all levels in the transition process. Solicit their input on improving customer interactions and recognise their role in delivering exceptional experiences. This involvement can foster a sense of ownership and reduce resistance.

- **Provide Training and Support:** Offer comprehensive training programs to equip employees with the skills needed for a customer-centric approach. This includes training on customer service excellence, communication techniques, and problem-solving strategies. Continuous support and resources can help employees adapt more quickly to new expectations.

Aligning Objectives

Develop a strategy that aligns customer satisfaction with business goals. Improving customer service can increase customer retention, driving revenue growth. Ensure that customer-centric initiatives are integrated into the broader business strategy.

- **Measure Impact:** Use metrics to assess the impact of customer-centric initiatives on business performance. Track key performance indicators (KPIs) such as customer satisfaction scores, Net Promoter Scores (NPS), and customer lifetime value (CLV). These metrics can help demonstrate the financial benefits of focusing on the customer.
- **Balance Resources:** Effectively allocate resources to balance customer needs and business goals. This might involve prioritising specific customer segments or initiatives that offer the highest return on investment (ROI). Regularly review and adjust resource allocation to ensure optimal outcomes.

YOUR ROUTE TO SUCCESS

Developing a customer-centric strategy involves integrating a customer focus into your entire business framework. Understanding your customers, creating a comprehensive customer journey map, empowering employees, leveraging technology, and fostering continuous improvement can ensure your business aligns with customer needs and expectations.

Understand Your Customers

Understanding your customers is the foundation of a customer-centric strategy. Invest time and resources to gather deep insights into their needs, preferences, and pain points.

- **Conduct Surveys and Focus Groups:** Regularly engage with your customers through surveys and focus groups. Ask questions to understand their experiences, preferences, and suggestions for improvement.

- **Analyse Customer Feedback:** Collect feedback from various channels, including social media, email, and in-person interactions. Use this feedback to identify common themes and areas to enhance the customer experience.
- **Develop Customer Personas:** Create detailed customer personas to represent different segments of your customer base. Include demographic information, behaviours, motivations, and challenges. Use these personas to guide your marketing, product development, and customer service strategies.

Create a Customer Journey Map

A customer journey map visually represents the entire customer experience with your brand. It helps you understand the customer's perspective and identify opportunities to enhance their experience.

- **Identify Key Touch Points:** Include all customer interactions with your business, from initial awareness to post-purchase support. Identify critical touchpoints where you can significantly impact the customer experience.
- **Analyse Pain Points:** Identify areas where customers may encounter challenges or frustrations. Use this information to prioritise improvements that will have the most significant positive impact on their experience.
- **Enhance Positive Moments:** Look for opportunities to delight customers at various journey stages. Small gestures, such as personalised thank-you notes or surprise discounts, can create memorable experiences that build loyalty.

Empower Your Employees

Your employees play a crucial role in delivering a customer-centric experience. Empower them with the tools, training, and authority they need to make decisions that benefit the customer.

- **Provide Comprehensive Training:** Ensure all employees, regardless of their role, receive training on customer service best practices and the importance of a customer-centric approach. This training should cover communication skills, problem-solving techniques, and ways to exceed customer expectations.
- **Encourage Ownership:** Empower employees to take ownership of customer issues and resolve them promptly. Trust them to make decisions that prioritise the customer's needs, even if it means going beyond standard procedures.
- **Recognise and Reward:** Recognise and reward employees who demonstrate exceptional customer service. This can include formal recognition programs, bonuses, or simply acknowledging their efforts in team meetings.

Leverage Technology

Technology can significantly enhance your ability to deliver a personalised and seamless customer experience. Implement tools and systems that help you manage customer relationships more effectively.

- **Customer Relationship Management:** CRM systems track customer interactions, preferences, and purchase history. This information allows you to provide personalised service and anticipate customer needs.
- **Data Analytics:** Leverage data analytics to gain insights into customer behaviour and preferences. Use this data to

tailor your marketing efforts, predict future needs, and identify trends that can inform your business strategy.

- **Automation Tools:** Implement automation tools to streamline processes and improve efficiency. Automated systems can handle routine tasks, such as order processing and follow-up emails, allowing your team to focus on more complex customer interactions.

Continuous Improvement

A customer-centric strategy requires ongoing attention and refinement. Review your plan regularly and adjust it based on customer feedback and performance metrics.

- **Monitor Performance Metrics:** Track key performance indicators (KPIs) related to customer satisfaction, retention, and engagement. Use these metrics to assess the effectiveness of your customer-centric initiatives.

- **Solicit Ongoing Feedback:** Continuously gather customer feedback through surveys, reviews, and direct interactions. Use this feedback to identify areas for improvement and make necessary changes.

- **Agile Approach:** Adopt an agile approach to customer-centric strategies, allowing flexibility and rapid adaptation to changing customer needs and market conditions. Encourage teams to experiment with new ideas, learn from failures, and iterate on successful initiatives.

- **Benchmarking:** Regularly compare your customer-centric practices against industry standards and best practices. Identify areas for improvement and innovation to stay ahead of competitors. Participate in industry forums, conferences, and networks to stay updated on the latest trends and innovations in customer experience management.

INSIGHTS FROM MY JOURNEY

For me, customer-centricity is all about truly understanding what my customers need, what they prefer, and the challenges they face. Once I know that, I can tailor my products, services, and interactions to meet and exceed their expectations. It's this deep understanding that drives real success in any business.

Over the years, I've seen firsthand how businesses that take the time to listen to their customers and understand their unique needs are the ones that truly thrive. In the car industry, for example, responding to customer feedback by developing new functionality or specifications made a real difference in staying ahead of competitors. Similarly, hospitality wasn't just about providing good service—it was about developing service models that anticipated guest needs and delivered exceptional experiences.

I've come to believe that the principle of *"the customer is always right"* should be replaced with a more forward-thinking approach: *"The customer should always come first."* This means constantly putting their needs in every decision, strategy, and interaction. Whether refining a product based on feedback or designing a personalised and seamless service, businesses that prioritise their customers' experience achieve long-term success.

27. CALIBRATING YOUR COMPASS

Companies that regularly assess and tweak their strategies aren't just reacting but staying ahead of the game. This proactive mindset is crucial for long-term success. Monitoring performance isn't just about tracking numbers but understanding their story. It's about spotting trends, identifying patterns, and making informed decisions that drive growth and improvement.

Businesses can foster a culture of accountability and agility by systematically planning, executing, and reviewing their actions. This cycle helps teams set clear objectives, implement strategies, measure results, and learn from their experiences. Transforming performance monitoring into a proactive process fosters innovation and excellence.

LEADING THE WAY

Netflix is a prime example of a company that has mastered the art of continuous improvement through performance monitoring and strategic adaptation. Since its founding in 1997 as a DVD rental service, Netflix has evolved into a global streaming giant known for its data-driven decision-making and ability to anticipate and adapt to changing market conditions.

Data-Driven Innovation

One of Netflix's key strengths is its rigorous use of data analytics to monitor user behaviour, preferences, and trends. The company collects vast amounts of data on viewing habits, which it uses to personalise content recommendations, optimise user experience, and inform content production decisions. Netflix continuously refines its platform by tracking metrics like user engagement, retention, and viewing patterns, ensuring customers receive relevant and engaging content. This data-driven approach has allowed Netflix to stay ahead of the competition and build a loyal customer base.

A Culture of Testing and Learning

Netflix is known for its culture of experimentation and continuous learning. The company regularly runs A/B tests to evaluate new features, interface designs, and content strategies, gathering real-time performance data to guide its decisions. This iterative process allows Netflix to test new ideas, learn from failures, and adjust based on user feedback. Netflix's flexibility and willingness to experiment demonstrate the importance of embracing change and learning from data.

Adapting to Industry Shifts

As the entertainment industry has evolved, so has Netflix. Recognising the limitations of the DVD rental model, Netflix pivoted to streaming in 2007. Later, the company foresaw the importance of original content production and launched its first original series, *House of Cards*, in 2013. Netflix has maintained its competitive edge by continually monitoring market trends and adjusting its strategy, even as new streaming services have entered the market.

Empowering Employees Through Transparency

Netflix fosters a culture of accountability and transparency, empowering employees to take ownership of their work and make data-driven decisions. The company's *"freedom and responsibility"* philosophy allows teams to innovate and take calculated risks while ensuring everyone is aligned with the company's strategic goals. Employees are encouraged to track their performance metrics and continuously improve, creating a high-performance culture that values agility and learning.

A Future-Forward Strategy

As Netflix looks to the future, it continues to invest in emerging technologies like artificial intelligence and virtual reality, ensuring that it stays at the forefront of industry innovation. By scanning the horizon for new opportunities and leveraging its vast data resources, Netflix is well-positioned to continue leading the entertainment revolution.

NAVIGATING THE WHY

Monitoring performance and reviewing outcomes are rooted in management science and organisational behaviour. These practices are essential for maintaining efficiency, effectiveness, and a competitive edge.

Feedback Loops

Regular performance monitoring creates feedback loops that help your business learn and adapt. These loops are crucial for identifying areas for improvement, reinforcing positive behaviours, and creating a continuous cycle of learning and enhancement. Employees who receive timely feedback can adjust their actions to better align with organisational goals, contributing to this ongoing process of action and feedback.

Decision-Making

Data-driven decision-making is a powerful tool that reduces biases and enhances the quality of strategic choices. By relying on accurate performance data, leaders can make informed decisions that align with their goals and improve outcomes. This is particularly important as cognitive psychology shows people are prone to overconfidence and confirmation bias. Performance data provides objective evidence to support decision-making processes.

Behavioural Insights

Understanding the behavioural aspects of performance monitoring can enhance its effectiveness. Positive reinforcement and constructive feedback based on performance data can motivate employees and foster a growth mindset. Research in psychology shows that individuals are more likely to engage in desired behaviours when they receive regular, constructive feedback.

Continuous Improvement

Businesses regularly monitoring and reviewing their performance are better equipped to implement continuous improvement strategies. This proactive approach fosters innovation and resilience. Constant improvement models like *Kaizen* emphasise the importance of small, incremental changes based on regular performance assessments. By consistently evaluating their processes, businesses can identify inefficiencies and implement solutions that enhance productivity and quality.

Accountability and Transparency

Clear metrics and regular reviews ensure everyone understands their responsibilities and the impact of their actions on overall goals. This transparency builds trust and encourages a culture of accountability. Employees are more likely to take ownership of their tasks when they understand how their performance contributes to the organisation's success.

Enhanced Strategic Alignment

Monitoring performance ensures that all departments and teams align with the organisation's strategic objectives. Regular reviews help maintain this alignment by providing opportunities to adjust strategies and initiatives based on performance data. This alignment is crucial for achieving long-term goals and sustaining a competitive advantage.

Risk Management

Performance monitoring also plays a critical role in risk management. Businesses can identify potential risks early and take preventive measures by continuously assessing performance. This proactive approach minimises the impact of risks and enhances the organisation's ability to navigate uncertainties.

IT'S NOT ALL PLAIN SAILING

Implementing a strong performance management system is essential, but it's not without its challenges. From data overload to resistance to feedback, maintaining effective monitoring and review practices requires strategic effort. By prioritising key metrics, fostering a culture open to feedback, and ensuring consistency in processes, you can build a robust system that drives continuous improvement.

Data Overload

Navigating today's sea of data can be overwhelming. Without a strategic approach, tracking too many metrics can lead to information overload, obscuring what truly matters for your success.

- **Prioritise Key Metrics:** Focus on identifying and prioritising the key performance indicators (KPIs) that significantly impact your business goals. Determine which metrics directly correlate with your strategic objectives and concentrate on those.

- **Use Visualisation Tools:** Data visualisation tools like charts, graphs, and dashboards can help you understand large amounts of information more clearly. These tools transform raw data into visual formats that are easier to interpret and analyse.

- **Data Governance:** A clear data governance strategy ensures that data is managed consistently and responsibly across the organisation. This strategy should outline how data is collected, processed, and stored and who has access to it.

Resistance to Feedback

Embracing feedback is crucial for continuous improvement, yet it often encounters resistance. Overcoming this barrier requires strategic communication and fostering a supportive environment.

- **Communication:** Explain how regular performance reviews and feedback sessions contribute to personal and organisational growth. Highlight success stories where feedback has led to positive changes.

- **Safe Environment:** Encourage open communication and ensure employees feel safe sharing their thoughts and suggestions. Implement anonymous feedback mechanisms if necessary to gather honest input.

Maintaining Consistency

Consistency in performance monitoring and review processes is critical to achieving reliable and comparable data. Ensuring that these practices are uniformly applied across your organisation can be challenging but is vital for effective performance management.

- **Establish Standard Processes:** Develop and document standard processes for performance reviews. This ensures that data collection, analysis, and reporting are consistently conducted, making performance data reliable and comparable.
- **Encourage Ownership:** Encourage employees to take ownership of their performance metrics. Provide them with the necessary tools and training to track their progress and identify improvement areas.
- **Performance Reviews with Goal Setting:** Regularly review and update individual and team goals to ensure alignment with overall business objectives. This integration helps keep everyone focused on what matters most.

YOUR ROUTE TO SUCCESS

Developing effective monitoring and review practices is like navigating a journey. You need a clear vision, the right tools, and the ability to adapt to changing conditions. By adopting a systematic approach and fostering a culture of continuous improvement, you can ensure your business stays on course towards its strategic objectives.

Set Clear Metrics

Setting clear metrics is the foundation of effective performance monitoring. It involves identifying the most relevant indicators to help you track progress and make informed decisions.

- **Define KPIs:** Identify the most relevant metrics to your business goals. Ensure these Key Performance Indicators (KPIs) are specific, measurable, and can be aligned with individuals' personal, positive, and present-tense targets.

- **Align with Strategic Goals:** Implement Objectives and Key Results (OKRs) to drive alignment with company goals and engagement. This alignment helps you track progress and make necessary adjustments to support your vision.

- **Adapt and Evolve:** Regularly reassess your metrics to ensure they remain relevant to your strategic goals. Be open to adjusting or adding new metrics to reflect changes in your business environment or objectives.

Implement Regular Reviews

Regular reviews are essential for keeping your performance monitoring efforts on track. They provide an opportunity to evaluate progress, identify areas for improvement, and make necessary adjustments.

- **Schedule Review Meetings:** Meet regularly to review performance data and discuss progress. These meetings should involve key stakeholders and focus on evaluating outcomes and identifying areas for improvement.

- **Use Data Analytics:** Data analytics tools are instrumental in gathering and analysing performance data. Dashboards and reports provide valuable insights into trends, patterns, and areas that require attention.
- **Involve Everyone:** Effective monitoring and review practices require a collaborative approach. Encourage team members to take ownership of their KPIs and contribute to the review process.

Leverage Technology

Leveraging technology is crucial for effective performance monitoring in today's digital age. Advanced tools and systems can streamline processes, enhance data analysis, and improve decision-making.

- **Invest in Analytics Tools:** Advanced analytics tools can significantly enhance your ability to monitor and interpret performance data. Business Intelligence (BI) software, predictive analytics, and real-time dashboards provide detailed insights into your operations.
- **Stay Updated on Trends:** Stay abreast of emerging trends and technologies in performance monitoring. Research and explore new tools, methodologies, and best practices regularly.
- **Automate Routine Monitoring Tasks:** Use automated tools to collect, analyse, and report data, ensuring your monitoring activities are consistent and timely. Automation frees up valuable time for your team to focus on strategic decision-making.
- **Leverage Cloud-Based Solutions:** Consider using cloud-based performance management solutions to enhance flexibility and scalability. Cloud-based tools allow you to

access performance data from anywhere, facilitate collaboration among remote teams, and scale your monitoring capabilities.

Utilise Collaborative Tools and Techniques

Collaboration is critical to effective performance monitoring. Collaborative tools and techniques can enhance communication, foster innovation, and ensure everyone is aligned with the business's strategic goals.

- **Enhance Communication Channels:** Utilize collaborative tools and techniques to facilitate open and transparent communication among team members. Implement project management software, instant messaging platforms, and virtual meeting tools.

- **Implement Cross-Functional Teams:** Create cross-functional teams to address specific performance challenges or improvement initiatives. Bringing together diverse perspectives from different departments fosters innovation and ensures that all aspects of the business are considered.

- **Conduct Regular Strategy Sessions:** Hold regular strategy sessions where key stakeholders can review performance data, discuss progress, and brainstorm new ideas. These sessions provide a platform for collaborative problem-solving.

INSIGHTS FROM MY JOURNEY

One of the most valuable lessons I've learned is the importance of regularly reviewing your direction—both as an individual and a business. Staying on track to achieve long-term goals requires constant assessment, recalibration, and the willingness to adjust your course when necessary.

A great example was a previous employer introducing a scorecard and meeting structure throughout the organisation. From top to bottom, every team and individual became focused on the critical deliverables for their specific part of the business. These metrics were directly tied to the overall company goals, ensuring everyone understood how their role contributed to the bigger picture.

This was one of the most straightforward changes, but it had a profound impact. It created a shared sense of purpose and accountability, and ultimately, it was a driving factor in the business regaining its number-one status in the industry. The company became more aligned, adaptable, and focused by consistently reviewing progress and making necessary adjustments.

This experience reinforced the principle of constantly reviewing one's direction of travel. It's not enough to set a strategy and hope for the best—continually assess where you are, where you're going, and whether any adjustments are required to stay on course.

AFTERWORD: NAVIGATING FORWARD

As we conclude *The Business Explorer*, I hope our journey has sparked fresh insights and empowered you to take bold strides in your business ventures. This isn't the end of your exploration—it's only the beginning. The tools, strategies, and mindsets we've explored together are your compass, guiding you through the ever-evolving business landscape.

REFLECTING ON THE JOURNEY

From the start, we focused on laying a solid foundation. In *The Golden Compass*, you learn to anchor your business with purpose, passion, and ethical leadership, identifying the core values that steer your decisions.

We then moved to *The Explorer's Toolkit*, where we equipped you with behaviours and mindsets critical to navigating uncertainty—including overcoming Imposter Syndrome, embracing a Growth Mindset, and cultivating resilience. All were designed to help you transform internal challenges into opportunities for growth and self-mastery.

In *Beyond the Horizon*, we shifted our gaze forward. You explored strategic planning techniques that prepare you to anticipate market trends, pivot swiftly, and lead with foresight. This wasn't just about surviving the future—it was about shaping it. By honing your ability to adapt and innovate, you've positioned yourself to thrive, no matter what the business world throws at you.

YOUR ROUTE TO SUCCESS

As you embark on the next phase of your business journey, remember that the principles we've explored together are tools designed to be lived, adapted, and applied. The real power lies in how you implement them. Take a moment to reflect: What strategies from this book resonated most with you? What new goals are you inspired to pursue? Write these reflections down, and start mapping your path forward.

Success doesn't come from standing still—it comes from constant exploration, adapting to new landscapes, and embracing the unknown with courage and confidence. As you continue your journey, remember that every decision you make shapes your business and its legacy.

NEXT STEPS: KEEP MOVING FORWARD

Now, it's time to put everything into action. The compass is in your hands, and the map is yours to draw. The business world is everchanging, and your ability to adapt, innovate, and apply what you've learned will define your success. Don't hesitate to revisit these pages, reflect on the insights, and use the lessons as you navigate new challenges.

The course you set today will influence the trajectory of your business tomorrow. Use the strategies we've discussed to chart your path and inspire others to follow. As you step forward, remember that the future belongs to those prepared to shape it.

CONTINUOUS GROWTH

To help you stay sharp and connected, here are some FREE resources:

Business Explorer Quiz

Unlock your potential! Scan the QR code and take on our *Business Explorer Challenge* to transform your business strategies. https://shorturl.at/Uou2t

Our Newsletter

Stay ahead of the curve! Get the latest insights, tips, and updates straight to your inbox. Scan the QR code to subscribe to our newsletter and start fuelling your growth journey today. https://shorturl.at/rAjLO

Connect and Follow Us

Don't miss out! For more inspiration, join our social media communities. Scan the QR code to connect with me on LinkedIn and follow us across multiple platforms. https://shorturl.at/hICak

ACKNOWLEDGEMENTS

First and foremost, thank you, the reader, for choosing to embark on this journey with *The Business Explorer*. Your time, curiosity, and commitment to growing as a business leader inspired this book. I hope the insights and strategies within these pages empower you to chart your course toward success.

A heartfelt thank you to my good friends Brad Parkes, who generously wrote the foreword for this book, and Ian Pilbeam for the thoughtful quotation gracing the back cover. Your contributions add so much value to *The Business Explorer*, and your friendship and support mean the world to me.

To my mentors, colleagues, and connections in the business world, your guidance has been invaluable. The wisdom you've shared, the challenges you've presented, and the encouragement you've given have all played a pivotal role in shaping this book and my approach to business and life.

A special thank you goes out to those who took the time to Beta test the content of this book. Your honest feedback, thoughtful critiques, and insightful suggestions were instrumental in refining the ideas and ensuring that *The Business Explorer* is as practical and impactful as possible. Your contributions have made this book better, and I appreciate your feedback.

Finally, the unconditional support from everyone who believed in this book, including my family, has not gone unnoticed. Your faith in this project kept me going through the late nights and the moments of doubt. Your encouragement has been the foundation upon which this book was built; I am endlessly grateful.

ABOUT THE AUTHOR

For 30 years, Dave Rogers has channelled his innate curiosity into business consultancy, coaching, and speaking, guiding businesses through transformative decision-making.

Dave's tenure with several FTSE companies honed his expertise, transforming it into actionable insights that empower teams to innovate and thrive. His strategic guidance propels businesses forward and positively impacts their communities.

As *The Business Explorer*, Dave brings collaboration, empowerment, and inspiration to every conversation, helping businesses overcome challenges and discover success-ready solutions.

He said, *"Witnessing my client partners exceed their aspirations and secure long-term success is incredibly rewarding"*.

Beyond his business ventures, Dave is deeply committed to mentoring students and advising schools on career strategies. He is a staunch advocate for community initiatives and proudly serves as Chair of the Board at The Kaleidoscope Plus Group, a leading mental health and wellbeing charity in the UK.

Printed in Great Britain
by Amazon